Advance Praise

Frank Macon's story has the feel of a grandpa sitting on the front porch telling his grandkids about a different time and place. There are stories of exploits fueled by a curiosity that helped Frank to learn about the world and himself. His curiosity prepared him for the life he imagined for himself. Young people who read this book will see how your life does not have to be perfect for you to become the person you were meant to be. This is more than the amazing story of how a young boy grew up to become an honored Tuskegee Airman. It is the story of how a life lived with perseverance can become a remarkable one.

— Rev. Eunice McGarrahan

Frank Macon's biography that chronicles his younger days is an authentic and compelling story of a young man born into hard times who achieves his dream of becoming a pilot and Tuskegee Airman. Macon overcomes many obstacles along the way through his own dedication, hard work, unwillingness to accept "no", and the love of an extended family. It is a book that has a great message for the youth of today. I heartily recommend it.

— Colonel Gene J. Pfeffer, USAF (Ret)
Historian
National Museum of
World War II Aviation

I Wanted to be a Pilot

I Wanted
TO BE A
PILOT

★ ★ ★ ★ ★ ★ ★ ★ ★ ★ ★

the MAKING *of a*
TUSKEGEE
AIRMAN

Franklin J. Macon
with Elizabeth G. Harper

NEW YORK

LONDON • NASHVILLE • MELBOURNE • VANCOUVER

I Wanted to be a Pilot

The Making of a Tuskegee Airman

Published in New York, New York, by Morgan James Publishing. Morgan James is a trademark of Morgan James, LLC. www.MorganJamesPublishing.com

The Morgan James Speakers Group can bring authors to your live event. For more information or to book an event visit The Morgan James Speakers Group at www.TheMorganJamesSpeakersGroup.com.

ISBN 9781683509608 paperback
ISBN 9781683509622 case laminate
ISBN 9781683509615 eBook
Library of Congress Control Number: 2018933116

Cover Design by:
Rachel Lopez
www.r2cdesign.com

Interior Design by:
Chris Treccani
www.3dogcreative.net

In an effort to support local communities, raise awareness and funds, Morgan James Publishing donates a percentage of all book sales for the life of each book to Habitat for Humanity Peninsula and Greater Williamsburg.

Get involved today! Visit
www.MorganJamesBuilds.com

To the ones who put up with me:
Mama, Aunt LaLa, Ol' Man Loper,
Cousin Ruth—who always told Aunt Maude—
and
The Warden Family

Love, Franklin

To Dad and Mom,
John and Sharon Blom
You gave me **_hope_**.
Love, Elizabeth

Table of Contents

FOREWORD

Do you ever dream an impossible dream? A dream so huge that it drives your waking moments, but you feel like the odds are stacked against you? A dream you are almost afraid to put into words because others will laugh. You keep your dream a secret and pour your energy into finding a way to move closer to that dream. A dream only you believe will come true?

Welcome to the club! I had an impossible dream as a child, and so did Frank Macon.

The odds were certainly stacked against Frank when he was growing up in the 1920's and 30's. Frank was raised by relatives and never knew his mother and father. He had severe dyslexia, which held him back in school as he struggled to read and was confused by numbers bigger than he could count on his fingers. He was continuously getting into trouble for pulling pranks or outrageous stunts, like careening down the street in a homemade rocket car using an old hot water tank, shooting flames like a gigantic torch out the back.

More than anything else in the whole world, Frank wanted to fly. He knew from a young age that he needed to make something of himself, and that "something" would be to become a pilot. For an African-American child at that time, this was indeed an impossible dream, but Frank would not give up.

His stories of mischief with carbide, jumping off the roof with homemade wings, learning about electricity the hard way, and driving the neighbor's car will leave you shaking your head in disbelief and laughter. And the discouragement he faced from teachers and others in authority who told him he would never do so much as wash and wax the cars because that was "his place" will probably make you angry and wonder that he could overcome the negativity which surrounded him. Anyone could be bitter after fighting against these odds, but that is not Frank's story. Instead, it is a delightful story of growing up with a dream and an unshakeable belief that he would find a way to make it come true. Against all odds, Frank did become a pilot and an aviation legend as one of the original Tuskegee Airmen.

Although we faced different challenges, Frank's delightful story of overcoming the odds and finding a way resonated with me. I grew up on the Mexican border in deep South Texas. My dream of flying in space was met with laughter, too. I also had a reputation for being more of a mischief-maker than a good student, but I wouldn't give up and eventually found a way to reach to the stars as a NASA astronaut.

I wish this book had been available to inspire me to overcome the odds, aim high, use my brain, never quit, and believe in myself.

Frank finishes the book by saying, "We made something of ourselves. If I can, then you can, too!"

Of course, he is talking about his fellow Tuskegee Airmen. They overcame impossible odds to soar above the clouds in service to our country. In the process, these great men quietly brought about change in our society.

The message is the same for everyone who dares to dream impossible dreams and is willing to work hard enough to make them come true.

I'm with Frank. If we can, then you can, too!

Michael E. Fossum
Colonel, USAF Reserves (retired)
NASA Astronaut (retired)
Chief Operating Officer/Texas A&M University Galveston,
Vice President/Texas A&M University

ACKNOWLEDGEMENTS

To the Colorado Springs Community that raised, educated, and supported Frank as he, despite great challenge, flew through history.

To Bristol Elementary, Washington Elementary, North Junior High School and Margret Bunger, and Colorado Springs High School (Palmer High School).

To Bill Thomas, Toni Miller, and the special collections team at the Pikes Peak Library District—Thank you for preserving history.

To Ms. Coyla Dowdell and Elizabeth's colleagues—Here's to double-stuffed Oreo hugs and silly string! And to the students at the Griffith Center for Children—May you, like Frank, overcome great challenges.

To Paul Batura and Tonya Lark—True professionals and friends.

To Greg Dyekman—Great appreciation for Joyful Tradition guidance.

To Terence James and Jaelyn Brown—Mr. Frank thanks you. He is very proud!

To the United States Air Force Academy Public Affairs Office— Gratitude for a birthday flight for a true American aviator.

To Astronaut Michael E. Fossum—Thank you for dreaming _**big**_ and reaching the stars.

To Rev. Eunice McGarrahan for wisdom, encouragement, and touching younger generations.

To Colonel Gene J. Pfeffer, USAF (Ret) —Thank you for preserving history.

To Dr. Kelly Woods—Thank you for getting Frank into the Palmer High School Hall of Fame.

To Bill Kennedy for all your support through the years.

To Tom Speed—Thank you.

To Chris Knapp and the guys at Bo Steel Fabrication & Structural Design, Inc.—Here's to tinkering, hovercrafts, and creativity.

To Bill Borders at the Western Omelette—Where everyone is family.

To W. Terry Whalin, Meredith Sloan-Hinds, and Sarah Costantino—Thank you for believing in our project and making it the best it could be.

To National World War II Aviation Museum, Colorado Springs, Colorado, and

Peterson AFB Air and Space Museum, Peterson AFB, Colorado—Thank you for keeping aviation history alive.

To Brighton Library District— A "Joyful" place to meet.

Special Gratitude

To Amy Lee—For all her love, help, and support.

To Richard Walker—Frank's lifelong best friend.

To friends Mark and Phyllis Dickerson—May we all learn to live honorably, love as God intends, and preserve history as the two of you.

To "Frank's experts"—Hannah and JB—May you always cherish your times with Mr. Frank and never forget to learn from those who came before you.

To Lew—My strength and support. I thank God for you each day.

To Deanna Dyekman and Stephanie Prescott, Joyful Traditions, LLC—My "Joyful" friends. Here's to dreams, family, friendship, and God's blessing! Without you this project would not have taken flight.

To sis—123 . . . 123, love you!

To Aunt Sarah and Uncle Craig—You made Colorado home. Thank you for **_all_**!

To dear friends Chris and Cindy Knapp—Where it all began!

Introduction

My name is Franklin J. Macon. Today, I am ninety-four years old. I didn't realize it when I was your age, but I was part of something big: ***history***!

Now don't you dare close this book just because I said, "history." I promise you will laugh.

I never planned it. At the "magic" age of ten, I carried a spit ball and a rubber band to all school assemblies. I drove Mama's car up the railroad bank and made my own orange crate airplane.

On Halloween, my friends and I placed dried leaves between the screen and the main door at the neighbors' houses. Back then, no one locked the doors. My job was to ring the doorbell and run. The air sucked the leaves right in the living room. Oh, what a mess.

Why did I do these things? I just thought, "Why not?" I got blamed for everything anyway. Let me tell you another thing. Guess who got the cleanup job? You guessed it. ***Me!*** I also got the spanking.

With all the shenanigans early on, no one thought I would one day become a pilot and an aircraft mechanic. But I did. I went to a famous flight school in Tuskegee, Alabama. I'll tell you more about that later.

Front of Frank's Tuskegee
Congressional Medal of Honor

Back of Frank's Tuskegee
Congressional Medal of Honor

Who would have dreamed I'd meet scientists, generals, and astronauts? Who predicted I would research airplane crashes, find the problem, come up with solutions, and save lives? Not a single soul, but I did exactly that!

After hearing all of that, you probably think I loved school. Actually, I **_hated_** school! When I was young, school was miserable. I didn't even like my birthday because of school. My birthday is August 4, 1923. I knew summer ended four short weeks after Mama cooked my birthday meal and Aunt LaLa made my birthday cake—angel food with strawberries.

I repeated second grade. Reading was terrible! My math skills were atrocious. That means really, really bad! I couldn't solve an arithmetic problem like this one in upper elementary:

3256
3256
+3256

I would add that problem fifteen different times and get fifteen different answers. Numbers moved around on a piece of paper like rabbits hopping around the woods. Letters jumped around on me, too. My classmates read like champs by second grade. I figured it out around seventh grade.

You see, ninety years ago, no one understood things like dyslexia. It's a learning disability that makes reading, math, and spelling very hard. I never knew I had it, but I did. It was just one of the many obstacles I had to overcome.

I preferred working with my hands. Paper and pencil tasks made me bored. Probably because I could not do them. If you are like me, I challenge you to use your hands and create some of the projects in the book.

School confused me, but that didn't mean I was dumb. Thankfully, I knew that. I fixed things. I made things. I was so curious at times it got me in trouble. Still, school, and what came with it, made people think I was just flat stupid. It really frustrated me. I remember Mama calling me a failure, which really hurt me for years.

It was the dyslexia that blocked my book-learning. It was dreadful. Some teachers tried to help me out. Mama and Aunt LaLa worked at helping me, too. The bottom line? It was up to me. I needed to work hard . . . ***very hard***. So, I did!

I decided to tell my story to encourage you. I want you to know that hardships happen. Oh boy, do they. But don't ever let it stop you!

Frank next to the plane flown for his 92nd birthday flight at
the United States Air Force Academy Airfield

The dyslexia caused me to get very bored with school. Looking back, I understand the boredom caused me to get into a little mischief. At times I wanted to quit, or at least skip school. Thankfully, I did not quit. Some adults thought I would never amount to anything. I proved them wrong.

Today people consider me a part of history. Many even call me an American Hero.

You see, I trained at Tuskegee. Before it was over, I was _**flying**_ . . . flying the AT-6!

But let me tell you, flying my AT-6 was the easy part. What I overcame to get there . . . now _**that**_ was a triumph.

Here is my story.

CHAPTER 1

Skeezix and the Parachute

My name is Franklin. Franklin with an "I." It used to be Franklyn with a "Y." Mama liked it that way. I wanted to be different, so I changed it. That was about third grade. I can tell you today the "Y" was different. As one who never liked following the crowd, I should have kept the "Y." Mama was right as usual.

Macon is my last name, but it should have been Banks. You see, "Mama" was really my great aunt. Her name was Maude Elizabeth Macon. Both of my great aunts' husbands passed away, so Mama and Aunt Ella moved in together. I called Ella "Aunt LaLa" because I always heard my birth mother, Eva, call her LaLa. The two great aunts took me in when I was two weeks old.

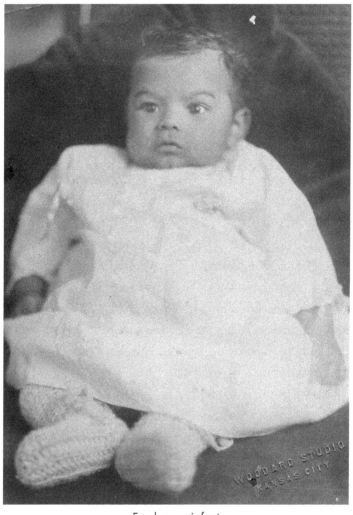

Frank as an infant

My birth mother was a young teenager; I think she was around fourteen when I was born. Her name was Eva Banks.

My aunts told me I was born in Kansas City, Kansas. I'm pretty sure about this, even though I never had a birth certificate. Well, I didn't until I had to prove my citizenship to go into the military.

Frank's birth mother, Eva Banks, as a young girl

My name was under "Births" in the family Bible. In those days, family records were kept in the family Bible. That information was as good as going down to the courthouse.

You might think I was totally confused. My name was even mixed up in the family Bible. You can see Franklyn Theodore and Franklyn James in our Bible. Who knows? Maybe Mama and Aunt LaLa picked a different name than my birth mother, Eva.

Family Bible (See Frank's name at the top)

I don't know who made the decision for me to go live with my great aunts. I'm pretty sure it was my birth mother. In those days, families got together and had big conferences about these things. Eva was just too young to take care of me.

We lived on Pine Street. I knew Eva, but I didn't realize she was my birth mother. I found out she was my mother when I was a teenager. I will tell what little I know about her.

I know Eva married a middleweight boxer named Ham Jenkins. They took me to Denver once in a while. I was little. I didn't know it was Denver, but it was. Ham and Eva swung me by my arms over the street curbs. They dressed me in an awful sailor suit. Eva and Ham bought me some little boxing gloves. Ham tried to teach me to box. It sure wasn't for me.

Eva Banks as a young woman

My other memory of Eva had to do with fireworks. I was around four or five. It was July 4th. I set off a couple of firecrackers on the front porch. I was playing with the matches I was not supposed to be touching.

Oh, Mama and Aunt LaLa shook their fingers at me. "Franklin, no more firecrackers. You'll blow the house up."

I launched the whole bag at one time. You should have seen the show.

Mama declared, "No more fireworks for you, Franklin!"

Eva heard this, and she was not having it. She spent a whole five dollars on new fireworks. She walked them down to our house and gave me the entire bag. It was fabulous. We launched every one of those fireworks that night.

Frank's only picture of Eva holding Frank

I don't even need to spend time telling you what kind of trouble I got in for that.

The last time I saw Eva was 1931 or 1932. I don't remember exactly. She remarried and moved away. She would write letters to me, and I would write her. No one told me she was my mother. Years later, she died. I'm not sure how. She was young when she died, so I never really got to know her. But I never lacked love. Mama and Aunt LaLa took very good care of me.

I am in my nineties now, so some things from my early years are hard to remember. I do remember my Skeezix. Skeezix was a popular doll in the 1920's. I guess my aunts thought that old Skeezix would be a favorite.

I was about four when Mama gave that old doll to me. I don't know where she and LaLa got the thing. I really didn't care for it. Then one day I figured out a perfect plan.

Each night, Mama would say, "Now get your Skeezix and take it to bed." If I didn't, she threw it in my bed anyway.

Mama made me wear my old footie Buster Brown night clothes, too. I didn't like those either, but they did come in handy for my Skeezix plan.

I figured out my Skeezix had pretty good aerodynamics. He parachuted beautifully. I got a hold of some cloth. I think I tore up a sheet. I made a parachute and tied it around my doll. I tossed it in the air. The doll floated down just as I planned.

I decided, "That's ok, but not too exciting." I needed more height.

I climbed right up on the house in my Buster Brown PJ's and threw that doll off the back porch. That's why my footie pajamas came in handy. I didn't need shoes, so I could sneak out of the house.

Yes, I climbed to the roof of the house.

The trouble was, after every throw, I had to crawl back down to the ground to get my parachute. If I wanted to launch my Skeezix again, I scrambled back up on the roof.

Being the innovative mind that I was, I hooked a long string to my Skeezix. I tossed it off the house. I stood right above my bedroom windows at the back of the house. I watched my Skeezix parachute to the ground. I hauled it back up again with the rope. I guess that old doll wasn't so bad after all.

People ask me today, "How did you get up on the roof?" Well, that was never any trouble for a creative young man like myself.

We had an old ladder in the garage. I put the bottom against the fence, so it wouldn't slip, and leaned the top against the roof. I climbed right up. The main roof pitched too steep, so I stuck to the roof of my bedroom.

The back porch was Frank's bedroom. Frank climbed this roof to launch his Skeezix doll.

Standing was more efficient than sitting. The parachute flew much, much better. I tossed that contraption in the air and let my Skeezix fly. I had hours of entertainment.

I engineered parachutes at an early age. I was good at it. You can do it, too. I learned to make those old parachutes and kites from hanging around the Warden kids. They were the older kids who lived next door.

When I was your age, a whole lot of adults thought a kid like me couldn't do anything creative. It wasn't because I had dyslexia; no one knew I had it. It was because of the color of my skin. They thought I would not be able to engineer a simple parachute. They also thought I would never be able to fly.

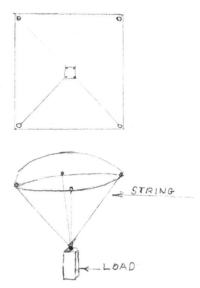

Parachute diagram drawn by Frank

You see, when I was two and a half years old, in 1925, the Army War College released a study. It stated that, because I was a Negro (that's what they said back then), I wasn't smart enough, honest enough, hard-working enough, and many other things. It said I really could not do much of anything.

Thankfully, I never listened to such ridiculous ideas. The Warden kids didn't, either.

I made all kinds of things, and so did the other kids in my neighborhood. We didn't pay attention to all of that nonsense. We built things all the time. We even tried to fly.

I'm proud to say my neighborhood was different from much of the country. It didn't have such problems. While much of the country fought the battles of segregation, our neighborhood worked together.

The kids, whether Black, Indian, Mexican, White, Chinese, or a combination of all the above, played _**together!**_ I'm not even sure we realized our differences. Really, that is the way it should be. Neighbor helping neighbor.

Now don't get me wrong—parts of town were definitely segregated. The movie theatre and the restaurants divided people by color and money. I never paid much attention because, as a kid, the places where I spent time, like school and the neighborhood, were not split. Believe it or not, it made me somewhat of an outcast when I went to flight school later in my life. It never occurred to me that I would not be allowed to do certain things due to the color of my skin.

Where I grew up, the only separation we had was at the beginning of the school day.

The girls had to go in one door at school, and the boys had to walk in the other door, but that was it. As soon as we entered the school, we all crowded together in the hallway. In class we sat in alphabetical order. Well, until I got moved to the front of the class, but that story is for another time.

Now, I am trying to remember the important people and events in my early years. Between the years of zero and four, Mama and LaLa were the most important. I also know the Warden family, who lived next door, changed my life.

Around age four, Aunt LaLa and Mama left me with Erma and Hazel, the Warden girls, when they went to work. The Warden family had been ranchers. Grandpa Warden even shot with the Buffalo Bill Wild West Show. That was a show where cowboys and Indians entertained people and showed them the way of life in the Old West.

If I recall correctly, Erma and Hazel taught me my ABC's and how to count. They were older, probably around twelve and fifteen. When you are four, you think that is really big stuff. They had a brother. His name was Bill. He liked building things and working on cars. I watched him like a hawk. The Wardens had an Uncle Bill, too. He was a little older, maybe two years older, than Brother Bill. I became interested in all things mechanical because I spent my time hangin' out with Uncle Bill and Brother Bill.

Erma and Hazel let me tag along with them in town, as well. Fortunately for me, the Warden girls had boyfriends. Boyfriends that worked. Lucky for me, they clocked in at the Alexander Aircraft Company. I remember the hangar. The factory opened in the Old North End of Colorado Springs just off Fillmore Street.

Factory of the Alexander Aircraft Company

Originally, Alexander was a movie-making company. The company wanted airplanes to deliver their advertising films. No one took them seriously when they ordered twenty-six airplanes.

What did they do? What any inventive minds would do. They started to build their own planes. They were so good at it, in 1928, Alexander Aircraft manufactured more airplanes than any other factory in the world.

The Warden girls dragged me up to Alexander Aircraft. Their boyfriends were pilots. They took the girls flying. They couldn't leave me alone on the ground, so I flew, too. That's right. No regulations back then.

I would be right up there with them, just soaring through the air.

That sure wouldn't happen today, but it did in the 1920's. A four-year-old on a pleasure flight.

Oh man, those planes fascinated me. I didn't understand that Eagle Rock airplanes from Alexander Aircraft and other planes were **_new_** inventions. The Wright Brothers took their first flight December 17, 1903, just twenty years before I was born. They flew 852 feet in fifty-nine seconds.

In 1927, very few people drove automobiles. Can you imagine how they felt about flying in an airplane? Mama and Aunt LaLa had a car. The car I remember was our 1929 Nash. They bought it when I was a little older. It had a green body with black fenders. Before we got our Nash, the Wardens drove Model A's and Model T's. That's where I learned to drive. Brother Bill and Uncle Bill plopped me on their laps in the middle of the car's front bench. They worked the peddles and the gears while I hung from the wheel to steer.

I was a kid so long ago our neighborhood shared only four telephones. We had one of the four. To distinguish your "ring" from the neighbors, you memorized the pattern. Our pattern was two fast rings and a space. Then it repeated.

To get our number, you lifted the handle to reach the operator.

She would say, "Number, please."

Then you asked for Main 4061R.

The neighbors had three fast rings. You waited for your ring pattern before you picked up the phone. Of course, all kids were tempted to listen in on adult conversations. You could hear anyone's conversation by picking up a phone.

I jump around a little when I tell about my life. I think it is because I have ninety-four years of stories to share. I will do my best to get them in some sort of order for you. Now, back to flight.

Airplanes frightened some people, like my Aunt LaLa. Flying didn't scare me one bit. It thrilled me.

Brother Hall from church once told me, "If people were meant to fly, they woulda' been born with wings."

Of course, I had a smart response.

I said right back, "If we were meant to wear clothes, we woulda' been born with them."

He just said, "Oh."

Brother Hall also wanted to know what would happen if you had a flat tire on your airplane while flying. Back then, the wheels didn't retract.

I said, "Pull up on a cloud and change it."

Brother Hall just said, "Oh."

Can you believe it? Brother Hall believed me.

Aunt LaLa and Mama, on the other hand, well, they knew I was being smart. Boy, did I get chastised about my fresh mouth for that comment.

Now, when the Warden girls brought me to the airplane hangar, I asked tons of questions. I asked so many questions a couple of the guys, Jimmy Donahue and Scotch Wysong, remembered me. They remembered me nineteen years later when I returned home from the military.

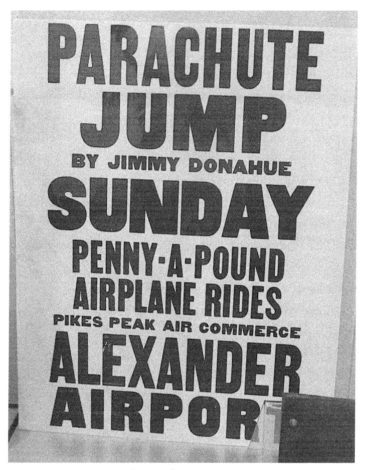

Jump advertisement

Jimmy Donahue was a pilot and a jumper. He held the high altitude parachute record for years. Scotch volunteered as a Flying Tiger when Japan invaded China before the United States entered World War II. We guessed Scotch joined because he was part Chinese and part American. His mom had been a missionary in China years before. More likely, he chose to fly because he was all aviator. If there was any chance of flying, Scotch signed up.

Curtiss P-40 Warhawk–Flying Tigers

Flight and airplanes captivated me. I wasn't alone. Charles Lindbergh prepared to make the first Trans-Atlantic flight May 21, 1927. The *Spirit of St. Louis* soared across the Atlantic in thirty-three and a half hours. With just one trip, Charles Lindbergh, nicknamed "Lucky Lindy," became famous from the United States to Europe.

Charles Lindbergh

I remembered hearing of this man, but I was busy making my own way as an aviator. It looked like all the odds were against me, even though I was only four years old.

I had dyslexia and didn't know it.

I was Black. It didn't matter to me, but it sure did to some in our Nation.

I could have used these obstacles as an excuse. ***No way!*** I refused.

I say there is no excuse for not making something of your life. I decided nothing would stop me. I was going to be a pilot.

Chapter 2

Ornamental Oranges and a Fried Egg

The same year that the Warden girls babysat me and took me to Alexander Aircraft Company, Mama, Aunt LaLa, and I headed to San Francisco. We were only there a few weeks. It was the first time we had traveled far away. We went back and forth twice to San Francisco by train.

Our first trip to San Francisco lasted just a short time. That's when Clara died. Clara was Eva Banks's mother. Remember, Eva was my real mother. Clara was also Mama and Aunt LaLa's sister.

We left San Francisco and went to Arizona for her funeral. She died July 13. Clara was my blood grandmother, but I had no clue. To this point, no one had told me Eva was my birth mother.

Mama, Frank, Aunt LaLa, and Clara

I was only four, so there was a lot I had no clue about. I didn't know my real mother and father, I didn't know I had dyslexia, and I didn't know there were many other brave aviators who paved a path before me.

Now, you probably know about Amelia Earhart. She is very well known, but I would like to tell you of another great aviator. Her name is Bessie Coleman. "Brave Bessie" was born five years before Amelia Earhart. She earned her pilot's license before Amelia.

Bessie helped her mother raise all twelve of her siblings. Her father left the family. Bessie's life was full of obstacles, but she never, never gave up. She educated herself and did exactly what her mother told her.

Her mother said, "Amount to something."

That is exactly what Bessie did.

Bessie Coleman's pilot license

On June 15, 1921, Bessie became the first female to earn her pilot's license. Not only was she the first female, Bessie was part Cherokee and part Black. She smashed down boundaries with sheer determination.

Bessie tried over and over to get flight training in the United States. She received a "*__no__*" at every turn. Bessie never, ever quit. Instead, Bessie taught herself French. She saved money, hopped on a ship, and sailed to France. There she learned to fly. She amazed audiences.

Bessie returned to the United States to "barnstorm" in airshows. That means trick flying. She changed flying in this country forever. Her dream to open a flying school seemed to end when she was killed in a flight accident on April 30, 1926. Later, others carried out her dream.

Bessie definitely "amounted to something." Aviators still remember her today.

I mention this because Bessie's death happened a couple of months before our travels to Arizona. You see, I was only four at the time, so I had no idea someone like Bessie Coleman would have an impact on me, but she sure did!

Bessie Coleman next to her Curtiss JN-4 Jenny

All these events in the world happened around me. Events are happening around you, too. I remembered the names but never thought they would have anything to do with me. My concerns were about exploring and tearing apart clocks and things like that. I was like most four- and five-year-old kids: curious.

It never occurred to me to pay attention to the world's events. I just wanted to blow things up with carbide. Occasionally, I wondered about my dad. I never knew him.

Well, I cannot really say that. I knew the man. He lived in the neighborhood. He had a wife and kids. Years after he was killed, I found out he was my biological father. But you see, he was never my dad. Some days it still hurts me. Everyone wishes their father was a good man. Mine, well, he did things I wish he hadn't.

When I think about it today, I think it would have been better if Mama and LaLa just told me about my real mother and father. They didn't. They tried to protect me from the family secrets. They meant well, but I still wondered, "Why don't I have a father? Other kids do."

At the age of four, I didn't dwell on the fact. Mama and Aunt LaLa loved me dearly, but I believe all children at some point want to know the truth about their biological parents. I never had that option. I was about twenty-eight years old when I figured out a man in town was my real father. He had been killed for things he never should have done. I put some clues and facts together to figure it all out.

My half-sister, Geraldeen, knew who our real father was years before I did. When I found out, Geraldeen and I became friends until her death. Geraldeen was the one good thing about that situation. The other good thing about my birth father was that he had great mechanical skills. I understand today that he gave me that gift. Of course, I had to practice my skills, but that natural ability came from him.

You know, stuff like that can tear at you. Yes, you will have to deal with it, but I'm gonna tell you straight forward: Don't let it stop you. I will tell you the same thing Bessie Coleman's mom told her, "Amount to something."

I questioned why I didn't have a dad, but I never questioned the mom part. I think it was because I always called my Aunt Maude "Mama."

I tried hard to listen to Mama and Aunt LaLa, but my curious brain just took over. Does that ever happen to you? I hope so.

That's how we learn new things. The same is true today. My curious brain gets me in trouble just like when I was a kid.

I have an old broken-down hovercraft that I'm working on. It keeps my brain busy even as we speak. I might be old, but I dream of sailing that thing over some water one day with my friends from the metal shop. I just know we will have a grand time!

Now back to being four.

Curiosity helped me follow my own path throughout my life, though it did lead to a few whippin's back in the day.

You see, in the 1920's, that's how it was. Children got whippin's. It was standard operating procedure. It was no big deal. Not a parent around worried about a kid's psyche. As a matter of fact, I don't think psyches had been born. No one knew anyone had one. The old saying was "Spare the rod and spoil the child." I believe that saying is true today, but a lot of people don't know it.

Looking too angelic for a spanking

Parents did know we had behinds. Any kid on Pine Street would have rather taken a punishment at school than getting it at home. Of course, if you got it at school, you got it at home, too. If your parents received a phone call or a note home, you were "in for it."

Families all grew switch bushes just for the occasion. In my case, it was a lilac bush. Aunt LaLa was my buddy, but she would whip me in a heartbeat. If I marched out to the switch bush and came back with a little tiny branch, then watch out!

I learned to pick just the right size. The switch needed to be long enough to please Aunt LaLa but short enough to spare my backside.

Mama disliked whippin', but she loved preachin'. Whenever I got caught doing something, Mama, she'd give me a big long speech. "Franklin, I didn't bring you up that way." She'd go on and on about that. She was good at those speeches. Sometimes I thought, "Just whip me and get on with it." She would make me get up at the piano and sing church songs. She decided that would straighten me out.

Well, the singing and spankings never worked. I still found trouble.

I figured it like this. When Aunt LaLa whipped me, if I howled too loud, she would say, "Boy, you ain't hurt one bit." If I didn't cry, Aunt LaLa said, "Franklin, you need another whippin' for things I ain't even caught up with."

Getting a spankin' in those days was a true art form.

Now, back to the story.

We took the train to San Francisco. Out West everyone could ride the train together. Of course, you could go First Class if you were rich. We were not, so we were in regular passenger cars. Now, this was very different years later when I headed to flight school in Tuskegee, Alabama. After we crossed the Mississippi River, they made all Blacks get on one car together. They even rearranged the order of the cars so the passenger cars with all White passengers were at the back of the train. You might think it would be the other way around. I thought it was ridiculous. They wasted so much time, effort, and money. It made no sense to me. The reason we were in the front of the train was that the coal ashes fell on the first car behind the engine.

Anyway, back in the West, years before that, Mama was a cateress. That means she cooked specialty foods for people. If I remember correctly, we traveled from Colorado Springs to San Francisco for the busy tourist season. When the hotels needed specialty foods for different events and holidays, they would hire Mama. We stayed a couple of months during the summer to make extra money.

Shortly after arriving in San Francisco, we got word of Clara Banks's death. Back on the train and off to Arizona for us.

When we arrived and finally got off that train, I saw these beautiful orange trees.

Mama told me, "Do not eat those oranges."

Well, you know what happened. I had to eat them. I did. I ate them. Trouble ensued. Those "ornamental" oranges were terrible, worse than a straight lemon . . . **_sour_!** I had no idea there was such thing as a decorative orange, but I learned fast.

I got sick.

Then someone said, "It is so hot you could fry an egg on the sidewalk." You guessed it. I did just that. I snuck an egg out of the house. Everyone was focused on Clara's funeral, but I concentrated on my experiment. I broke that egg. I cooked it on the sidewalk. You know, it worked. Thankfully, I learned from the oranges. I didn't eat the egg.

CHAPTER 3

Kindergarten and Chugs

We left Arizona and returned to Pine Street in Colorado. I turned five that August.

Shortly after our time in Arizona, Mama and Aunt LaLa bought me a little violin. I guess they wanted me to be cultured or something. Well, I hated that thing.

My teacher lived down the street. I marched down Pine Street to his house for each lesson. One day he told my aunts, "That boy is awful."

He said, "This boy ain't never going to learn the violin."

I said to myself, "You got that right. What in the world do I want with this thing?"

Now, I knew better, but I decided, "If it upset the teacher . . . ***good!***" I should have been upset, but I thought it was great! Got me out of violin lessons.

I looked good in my violin picture, but the sound. Let me tell you.

Frank and his violin

The squeakin' and squawkin'. I pulled the bow over the strings, and it was just awful! That sound could wake a hibernating bear.

I tell you this because it is important. Every one of us has different abilities and talents.

You see, for some, playing an instrument—it is the best thing ever. If you are good at it, keep it up. For me, it was **_not!_** I would rather have played in the dirt or in the coal shed. The shiny gold specs on lumps of coal fascinated me more than the violin. I dug out the flecks of gold. I thought I'd be rich. It took years before I learned those gold specs were simply iron pyrite or Fool's Gold. It only took five violin lessons for me to know I was terrible.

I figured if I got rid of the violin, I'd be better off. I walked up the street to my cousin Bob Anderson's house. Bob was Aunt JuJu's grandson, and Aunt JuJu was Mama's sister-in-law. I gave Bob my violin. Aunt JuJu ratted me out to Mama. My two old aunts marched me straight back to Bob's house. They snatched that old violin right back.

Don't get me wrong. Just because I was awful at the violin doesn't mean I don't like music. I do. I thoroughly enjoy music. The classics and the old folk music like "John Henry the Steel Driving Man." Sons of the Pioneers were one of my favorite groups.

You see, when I was five, the people who lived a couple doors down were cowboys. True cowboys. They sang around that old camp fire and drank coffee as thick as tar. If you ever got a touch of their skin, it was tough as leather. To me they were kind of like real-life heroes. That's saying something because I'm not what you would call a hero-worshipper—it takes a lot to impress me. When I was five, my heroes were Buck Rogers and aviators.

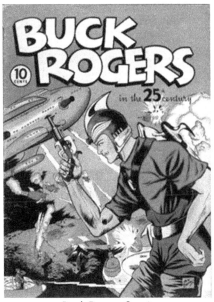

Buck Rogers Comic

It was 1927, and Prohibition was going on. That's when the federal government made liquor illegal. ***For everyone!*** The trick in our neighborhood was to disguise that old liquor.

On one side of the cowboys' house lived a policeman. Two doors up was another policeman. Now, some of these people in the neighborhood made some kind of bathtub gin or whatever it was called. Even though it wasn't legal to drink alcohol, the neighborhood was making it. That's what Mama told me. These old cowboys sat outside and sang the old cowboy songs. They were distracting the police from the bathtub gin-making, I guess.

You know I never saw those old cowboys drink anything but that tar coffee. I never paid much attention to the liquor. I chose not to drink at a very early age. I watched too many men drink their lives away. Looking back, I made a great choice.

When I was five, I loved to sing with those cowboys. I stayed all night if I could. I learned most of those tunes. Except there was one I hated that those old cowboys started singing. It was "Little Joe the Wrangler." It was so sad. Joe fell of the cliff, and his horse fell on him. I thought it was the saddest song. I started crying so hard. I ran home.

That's how those old wranglers got rid of me at night. Now "Ol' Shep," I learned that one from them, too. It's a favorite.

My music appreciation came from those cowboys and Bristol School, where we had to listen to something called *The Walter Dam Rush Hour*. The teachers made us listen to *The Walter Dam Rush Hour* all through elementary. It was a radio show. They played classical music every Wednesday for an hour. The whole school sat on the gymnasium floor, listening to the classical music. You can just imagine my friends Brother and Buster and I sitting on the gym floor for an hour. Yes, a full hour. No moving, no talking. Well, we did move a little. We tried to shoot a few spit balls. That wasn't the best idea we ever had.

It sure was tough sitting there, but I still have a great appreciation for classical music thanks to that old radio show.

I had one other music teacher, and that was Mama. She taught me the spirituals. To me, the old spirituals, those are songs that come from the heart. I learned those songs from her. I will never forget them. They were workin' songs. She sang the old time gospels, too. She belted those things out with heart. Oh, "The Old Rugged Cross," now that one's a little too sad for me, but I do love "Amazing Grace."

Age five was the year of music for me. Shortly after the five violin lessons, my two old aunts gave me piano lessons. I learned **one** one-handed song.

The piano teacher said to Mama, "He ain't never gonna learn."

I said, "You got that right!"

Today, I kind of wish I could play the piano, but I'm not losing any sleep over it.

You see, I wanted nothing to do with the violin or piano. At the time, I wanted two things: I wanted to play the guitar, and I wanted to fly.

Aunt LaLa, who was very religious, said, "He ain't learnin' guitar. It's the Devil's instrument."

Grumman F4F-4 Wildcat, NASM Cockpit

Oh man, that made me want to play the guitar even more.

I did get into singing. I learned all the church songs. It helped me get out of a few whippin's with Mama. All this happened in the summer. Little did I know my fun would come to a screeching halt.

It was 1928.

Jimmy Doolittle flew the first flight using only instruments. He took off and landed without problem. Unfortunately, I was about to have a problem. It was called ***school!***

I thought school would be interesting. It wasn't. I had hung around all the older kids in the neighborhood. They taught me my ABC's and numbers, so why should I sit around and learn something I already knew? I watched the older kids fix cars. I climbed the roof to throw my Skeezix when the babysitter paid no attention. I flew in an airplane at the Alexander Aircraft Company. Writing your ABC's and sitting in a desk is just not as exciting as flying. And it is not as fun as driving the neighbor's car. I was a year older, but I still couldn't sit in the seat and touch those pedals. The Warden boys thought it was funny.

I anticipated great things when I started school. I expected kindergarten to start out with the principles of flight or something. You know, exciting stuff. I wanted to do experimental projects. After all, that was what we did in the Warden's garage. We tested those Model A's. We tore apart the engine. We pulled apart the springs. We dismantled the carbide headlights.

We didn't stop with the cars. We took the wheels off our wagons to make chugs. We usually used our wagon wheels. Back then, our wagon wheels were wooden. Some of the wagon wheels were wood, and some were real fancy. The seat was part of the orange crates from Benton's Grocery. The rope handle—well, sometimes we had to use part of a clothesline. I would not suggest this option. You would get a whippin' for cutting the clothes line. A few years later, we added the old gas engines from our wash machines to our chugs. You can't do that today because wash machines don't run on gas engines.

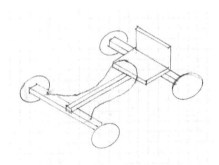

Frank's drawing of his chug

Chugs were great. Especially for young boys and a couple of girls, like my cousin Ruth, who lived on the East Side. Our roads were perfect chug tracks, all dirt. We started up by Manitou Garden, which was part of the "Foothills." We raced as fast as we could. If you held your feet on the crossbar, you made great time. The goal: make the turns without wiping out or hitting a street car. First one to arrive safely back on Pine Street was the day's champion.

We steered with our feet. Oh man, you better wear your shoes. The only brakes around were the soles of your sneakers. It was always great fun until someone burned a hole in their shoe trying to slow down their chug. After all, shoes were a luxury in the 1920's. Now that I think about our chug races, it is a miracle no one hit a street car.

I always wanted to learn how things worked. How clocks ticked. How airplanes flew. I wasn't so keen on learning about Dick and Jane and their dog, Spot, in the boring classroom books. I had great plans in my brain, but I just couldn't understand what they were teaching me at school. I did not learn the way they taught. My brain lacked the ability to read. Paper and pencil work was almost impossible.

I could learn alright, but I learned in a very different way. Forget the paper and pencil; let me build or do something with action. Then I never forget what I am taught.

I tried to figure out electricity. Lights amazed me. How they turned on and off. I didn't read about it—I hooked things up to the electricity. **_Zap!_** This is not recommended. I'd get shocked and blow out the fuse. I learned not to do that again. Not so smart, but I learned how that electricity worked.

Old-fashioned electrical fuse

Fixing the electricity was another story. Today you can simply flip a fuse switch, and the electricity comes back on. Not so in 1928.

Back then, families had these screw-in fuses. Mama had to call the utility company to come out and put in a whole new fuse. I attached so many objects to the electrical system I got Mama in trouble with the electric company.

Now, for Mama, the electricity was sacred. She did not want anyone to touch the switches. The Wardens, on the other hand, were like me. We made all kinds of contraptions using electricity.

The utility company told Mama, "Keep that boy away from that electrical system, or we will turn off your electricity." Thankfully, they never turned off our power. Mama must have sweet talked 'em or cooked them some good food.

I never got to mess with the fuses at school. Back then, kindergarten was a half day. I played in the sand pile. We made little Pilgrims and Indians out of clothespins and stuck 'em in the sand.

"Come on!" I thought. "This does not interest me at all."

Teachers fed us milk and graham crackers. Now, I am very allergic to milk. Back then, no one paid attention to allergies, either. I threw up if I ate the snack, but I received a spanking if I didn't. It was quite a dilemma until Dr. Timmons wrote a letter to the school: "**_No more milk!_**" From that day on, I brought goat's milk.

My teacher made us take naps. It was terrible! I figured I could go home and go to bed. For me, being still was almost impossible.

"Let's get something going!" my brain shouted.

I liked to be on the move so much I believed spankings were a far better punishment than having to go to my room and go to bed. Being sent to my room was like the end of the world. A spanking was even better than having to sit still with nothing interesting to do. So, naptime at school was terrible.

While I was in kindergarten, Eva still lived in town. Remember, she is my birth mother. When I started school, Eva tried to help me with my arithmetic. She gave up and made me count on my fingers because I couldn't count in my head. It was the dyslexia.

Eva, age 7

That worked ok for a while, but when it came to seeing numbers on paper, I would get all confused. I realized, years later, the downfall to using my fingers all the time was that I stopped memorizing math facts.

I committed math facts to memory many years later. I highly suggest you memorize your math facts. Even if it is hard, figure out a way to get those numbers in your brain. It will pay off when you are older.

Eva steamed when I made math mistakes. That's because she was extremely good at math. I, on the other hand, just could not do number problems. Reading was just the same . . . **_hard!_**

As kindergarten went along, I began to realize I got more out of looking at pictures. Reading was just too difficult, so I started to train myself to listen. I never got any meaning out of reading, so I had to figure something out.

Chapter 4

Fortunes, Feasts, and Getting Even

School continued to be hard, but that didn't stop the neighborhood fun. My classmates learned to read. I learned that "b," "d," and "p" all looked the same. Not to mention "6" and "9" and "2" and "5." The letters and numbers jumped all over a piece of paper. I completed kindergarten and started first grade, but learning did not get more exciting. I had to look for fun elsewhere.

Let me tell you a little about my friends Buster and Brother.

My friend Buster Moss, well, his real name was John. He was my cousin. Brother Moore's name was Isaac, but no one, not even the teachers, called him Isaac. We walked to school together every day. I don't think they had trouble with reading and arithmetic. As an adult, Buster went to California. He moved away after World War II to Oakland, California, I think. He worked for the post office. Brother became an attorney and State Representative in

Denver, Colorado. I tell you what. I don't remember some things, but I do remember a few tricks we played.

Now let me just say our kind of trouble was never serious. We loosened the valve stem of tires to allow the air to escape. It wasn't to be mean. We wanted to watch to see how the valve worked. Today you get in real trouble for stuff like that. Back in my day, it was just cause for a whippin' if you got caught. Let me tell you, we always got caught!

One of our favorite tricks was to jack up the rear axle of neighborhood cars and place a block under the axle so the rear wheels were slightly off the ground. The wheels spun, but the car would not move. We learned that one from the older kids. That little trick doesn't work today with automatic cars.

The older kids in the neighborhood let Old Man Reed's cows out. Those old cows ended up on the railroad bed. The whole neighborhood helped retrieve them. Every last one of them. Like I mentioned earlier, the whole neighborhood chipped in when someone was in need. I can't tell you how many times Ol' Farmer Reed harnessed up his work horses to pull a stuck car out of the mud.

Buster and I were about the same age. He was quiet and nice, but he had an ornery streak. Whether we did it or not, Brother and I got the blame. Not Buster.

Oh man, did he do stuff. Buster's angelic looks saved him, though. He mastered schmoozing or sweet-talking his way out of trouble. One time, Buster got some of his father's cigars and brought them over to our garage. We all had a puff. I got so sick I think I turned green. I have never to this day smoked another cigar or cigarette.

We all carried a little devilish streak. The older neighborhood kids mentored us. We watched their schemes, then we created our own. Those older boys put .22 caliber bullets in the old potbellied stove in the church. An unsuspecting adult started a fire with those bullets sitting in the stove. It took just the right amount of time for those bullets to heat up. When the stove was good and hot, and the sermon good and long . . . **_pop, pop, pop!_** Bullets exploded like kernels of corn.

Those older boys knew the church prayed for the Holy Spirit to come down. They helped with this, too. To bring a little pizazz to the prayer request one day, the older boys placed several pigeons in the church attic. The attic had a trap door. Just as the reverend called for the Holy Spirit, those older boys sprang open that door.

Chaos ensued. The old ladies screamed, and Aunt LaLa laughed from her toes. Those boys ran. Even Jesus wasn't saving them from a swat that day.

Even though I caused trouble, I had Mama and Aunt LaLa to keep me in check. Mama, she carried herself with dignity. Mama concerned herself with my wellbeing.

Frank, Mama, and Aunt LaLa

Mama said, "Franklin, sit up." "Franklin, I didn't teach you to have a fresh mouth." "Franklin, you know better than that." Before I left the house each day, Mama made me say, "In every day and in every way, I'm getting better and better."

I ran out of the house into the street and hollered, "In every day and in every way, I'm getting worser and worser."

Aunt JuJu, who lived down on the corner, heard me. She trudged straight over to Mama's and ratted me out.

"Maudella (that was Maude and Ella combined—she always said their names together), did you hear that boy?" I got in trouble for that, too.

Aunt LaLa was spiritual. Real churchy. One time when we were in San Francisco, she saw a plane write in the sky. Aunt LaLa never saw such a sight. She thought it was the good Lord sending her a direct message.

"Franklin, the Lord's sending us a message."

The plane was skywriting an ad for Pepsi Cola.

I said, "When did the good Lord learn to spell 'Pepsi Cola'?" She almost knocked me to the next block.

Aunt LaLa was serious about God and church. Once you met her, you knew. She was just as serious about fun. And discipline.

Aunt LaLa spent most of her day in the backyard. She planted and weeded the garden. She whacked chickens on a stump and soaked off the feathers so we had dinner. Back then, you butchered your own. I hated those chickens, but not Aunt LaLa. Not one hesitation. She grabbed a chicken by the neck and **_wham!_** That was how we always had food on the table.

Then there was Aunt JuJu. She lived down the street, on the corner of Pine. Mama's first husband, James Macon, was JuJu's brother. She was the character of all characters.

JuJu was part Cherokee Indian and part Black. Every day she left the house with her beads and her cane. I remember the turquoise half-moon the best. Those jewels and beads dangled around her neck down to her waist. At least ten pounds of 'em, or so it seemed. Aunt JuJu made dandelion wine by the barrel. It was Prohibition, but that didn't stop her. She drank and shared what she brewed.

On top of all that, JuJu told fortunes. That's right. She even had fortune-telling cards. Her daughter used a crystal ball.

Those rich folks over in the Broadmoor wanted to know when their money was coming back. The Depression took it, you know.

That's how Aunt JuJu made a living. Believe it or not, the Depression was actually good for Aunt JuJu. Now, I won't mention some of the tricks she pulled on those fortune-seekers. I'll leave that to your imagination.

Aunt JuJu once told me my fortune. I was in first grade. It didn't mean a thing. Many years later, when I was over at her house, Aunt JuJu sat me down. She was serious.

"Now, boy, you listen to me," she said. She repeated almost the same fortune from my childhood. "You are going to survive something terrible."

My analytical mind paid no attention. "Ha!" I thought to myself. Shortly after, I survived a helicopter crash.

Aunt JuJu always said I had a protection around me. I guess she was right. I didn't crash one day in flight school when the winds were so strong my classmates all thought I was going down. I made it back from the inverted spin that turned me white as a ghost. That's saying something. I survived a helicopter crash at Fort Carson. I guess crazy old Aunt JuJu was right on target.

While I was six, I was in first grade. It was just as the country was going into the Great Depression. It was also the year William

J. Powell founded the Bessie Coleman Flying Club out in Los Angeles.

While serving in World War I as an infantry lieutenant in the U.S. Army, Powell was badly wounded by poison gas. Like many other brave aviators, his hardships never stopped him. Eventually he started an airplane factory and wrote a book called *Black Wings*. It not only encouraged young aviators to fly, but also to become aircraft mechanics like me.

William J. Powell

We were talking about the Depression. My family, from what I remember, did alright during the Depression. Now, we were definitely not rich, but we always had food, shelter, and clothing.

Mama always fed us. My other aunt, JuJu the Fortune Teller, well, she fed the neighborhood. JuJu made all this money telling those rich folks fortunes. Ol' JuJu made a killing making dandelion wine, too.

Aunt JuJu would send Stanley, Buster, or Larry down to Benton's grocery store to buy up all the hamburger and some beans. They were my cousins. They'd go to the store with the money she got from her fortune telling.

Back then, a dollar practically bought a whole cow. Maybe not a whole cow, but it sure bought a lot of hamburger. Aunt

JuJu got out there in the backyard. She cooked that meat over an open fire. She added spices and beans to the mix. Next thing we knew, her giant cauldron boiled with chili. Aunt JuJu stirred and stirred. When the chili was just right, we placed that cauldron in our wagon. Buster and I carted it all over the neighborhood. The neighbors filled their bowls full of JuJu's chili. During the Depression, I always said, "JuJu and Father Divine fed the neighborhood." Father Divine started soup kitchens all across the country during the Depression. JuJu stuck to our neighborhood, but she did a good job, too.

Kerosene was probably about three cents, but I remember it being five cents a gallon. That was a significant amount of money in 1929. I also remember Mama called down to Benton's Grocery.

She'd say, "I want several pounds of dog meat."

I remember going down to Ol' Man Benton's Grocery. Dog meat meant a whole lot of bone and a little bit of leftover meat. Mama stretched that "dog meat" into tasty soups to feed the family. When she squeezed all the taste and goodness from the bone, she tossed the bones out to our dog, Boots.

The Jewish families in town booked Mama up a year in advance for her cooking. She was that good. She made all kinds of special holiday foods. She learned from her first husband, James Macon. Remember, he was JuJu's brother and a chef. He hunted often. He taught her how to cut and prepare meats. If she went to the butcher shop, she instructed them.

Those butchers loved to have her. She was tremendous at her trade. Mama fixed all kinds of meat. She knew how to prepare venison, rabbit, and other wild game. Mama was terrific at cooking the main course, but she wasn't so good at cakes. Thankfully, Aunt LaLa prepared those.

Mama was good with greens. She cooked the greens to perfection. She knew the trick. She took those greens out before the water turned color.

She said, "You lose all the vitamins that are good for you. You might as well drink the 'pot liquor' because that is where all the vitamins are."

Wild rice or Indian rice, as it was sometimes called, round

steak, spinach, and lemon pie. Those were my favorites. I liked strawberry shortcake, too, but not with biscuits. I enjoyed it with angel food cake. That's how Aunt LaLa baked it for me. Mama cooked my favorites if I made it through the day without a whippin'. Believe it or not, I actually made it a couple of times.

I tell you this because food was very important during the Depression. To get your favorite meal was quite a treat. It was also a treat to get a new pair of shoes. The shoes I remember the most were

Shoe X-ray machine like the one at Voorhees Shoe Store

my new Easter shoes in first grade.

Every Easter it was customary to buy new clothes for the Easter church service. Of course, as a child, you were expected to perform in the Easter service. I had to recite.

Well, I had last year's Buster Brown high tops. I hated them. I wanted the low quarter shoes. Those are regular shoes, not high top shoes. I thought I was a man. After all, I was in first grade. I wanted low quarters.

Voorhees Shoe Company was where Mama and LaLa bought all our shoes. They bought me a pair of shoes for Easter. To start off the story, *yes*, I got in trouble!

I thought, "Oh man, they're going to get me high tops again." We were at Voorhees, and they brought those low quarters out. "Oh man!" I wanted those shoes. They toted out the only size they had. Two sizes too small.

I had my toes all crumped up in there.

I decided, "I am going to get these shoes no matter what."

In those days, you put your foot in an X-ray machine to see if shoes fit. They outlawed those machines a long time ago due to too much radiation.

The salesman said, "They won't work."

I still talked them into it. Mama and LaLa bought the low quarters.

Easter Sunday, off to church we went. The shoes hurt me ***bad!*** In church I wanted to take them off.

Mama said, "Ok."

But Aunt LaLa shook her finger, "Oh no, you aren't. You're leavin' em on. That will teach you, boy, a lesson."

I stuck my tongue out at Aunt LaLa. That was a mistake. Boy, she whacked me so hard I almost went over the back of the pew. I started to cry.

"Don't you make a sound." She mentioned "outside" and "beating to a pulp." At that time, I did not know what pulp was, but I was about to find out!

She said, "Don't you stick your tongue back at me."

Let me tell you, I never did that again!

Next day, Mama took the shoes back to the store. Later, I did get the shoes I wanted in the right size.

The new shoes weren't good enough for me. I decided it was time to get even with Aunt LaLa. I created a great plan. We had an ice box. The ice wagon would come and bring bricks of ice, and we would chop hunks of ice off for drinks.

So, I said to myself, "Self. If I chop off a little of this ice, when LaLa goes to bed and she goes to sleep, I'll ease some of this ice up around her feet."

I had tried to get even with her before. I stuck her hairbrush up under her covers. I think she thought she did that, so I never got a reaction. Well, let me tell you. The ice worked!

I kept myself awake until I knew Aunt LaLa was sound asleep. I tiptoed into the kitchen, used the ice pick to retrieve my hunk of ice. I snuck into her room. I eased that ice up around her feet. I don't know how she knew it was me. I calculated the rate of ice melt and distance to LaLa's feet. I had a good seven minutes to run on the porch back to my room and fake sleeping.

I pretended to be asleep. Before I knew it, Aunt LaLa pounced on top of me. All fours. ***Bam!*** She pinned me down. That wasn't such a good idea, either. I got it for that one, too.

Around this time, I thought I was brilliant. I thought, "I'm getting even with Mama and Aunt LaLa. I'll show them."

I did this a lot when I was coming along. I wrote a note in my best handwriting. It stated, "I, Franklin Macon, am running away."

I couldn't wait to see the fear in their eyes. I hid under the bed and listened. Aunt LaLa discovered my note. She read it to Mama.

I assumed they would cry and boo hoo all night.

They must have known I was hiding under the bed.

Mama said in her best stern voice, "Well, Ella, we better call the police."

I heard "police." I jumped from under that bed so fast I about knocked myself flat. Once again. Getting even. Not such a good idea.

Getting in trouble was a hazard of being a six-year-old boy. If someone dared me to build a rocket ship like Buck Rogers, I did just that. It didn't matter that I might set the yard on fire. That didn't concern me. Back then, I thought I knew everything. Now, I know. You're not as smart as the old folks. You just think you are.

CHAPTER 5

Chores and Other Scary Things

I headed toward second grade. School was still very hard. What I didn't know at the time was that life was even more difficult for most of the country. The Crash of 1929 destroyed the economy. If you didn't have a skill, life was tough. Maybe that's why I always knew to stay in school.

I had work besides classwork, too. Mama gave me chores the day after I was born.

Well, not really, but I don't remember a time when I didn't have chores. I scooped up the ashes from the fire. I washed dishes. I chopped wood. I cleaned out the chicken coop. Oh, that was the worst! I detested those chickens. The smell was awful! Almost as bad as the stinky outhouse on a hot summer day. Those chickens ran all around. They scared me to death. Aunt LaLa, of course, thought this was great. She grabbed any chicken that got close to her without even blinking. The funny thing was that Aunt LaLa was scared to death of the dark, but she would take on a crazy chicken any day. If we needed meat for dinner, well, you know what happened. Aunt LaLa marched out back, opened the coop, and snagged a poor chicken by the neck. Next thing you know, **_whack!_** We had dinner.

The chicken coop–Location of Frank's first "unsuccessful" solo flight

About a year into the Depression, the hobos came. They rode the train that ran right behind our house.

Asking for help was different back then. No one took handouts. Everyone had too much pride. If you needed food, you offered to work.

At our house, Mama fixed sandwiches for the hobos. Most rode the train from the East. In return, the men chopped wood. That annoyed me. I thought chopping wood made me a man. It was the one chore I liked. It built muscles.

I didn't want those hobos doing my job. I wished Mama would have them wash dishes. Better yet, I wished they cleaned the chicken coop.

The country suffered in more than one way. We were unknowingly between World War I and World War II. Of course, I had no idea. I had other troubles. Chickens, my cousin Ruth, and school.

Ruth (left-hand picture). Mama, Aunt LaLa, Ruth, and Frank in Garden of the Gods. Frank is not happy.

I decided I had better figure out this reading thing. Every time I brought a note home from the teacher, I got a swat or a scolding. Mama sat me at the piano. We sang the old spirituals. She had me say, "Oh Lord, if I have wounded any souls today, forgive me."

My trouble was not the singin'. I had no idea what that note from school said. I'm quite sure one had to do with the pepper I put inside of my second grade teacher's chocolate-covered cherries. It all started when I got moved to the front of the class. My teacher made me sit up front, right next to her desk. I decided to get even. I should have known from my plan to ice Aunt LaLa's toes that getting even is not always the best choice. But you know, I was a seven-year-old boy. As a seven-year-old, you don't always think these things through.

A classmate gave my teacher a box of chocolate-covered cherries. I think it was for Christmas. I sawed a little circle in the bottom of each cherry. I delicately pulled the circle of chocolate off the bottom. I scooped out the cherry and poured in the pepper. To cover my work, I placed the cherry and chocolate circle very carefully back into the bottom of the candy. I smoothed out the chocolate, and I set them gently back in the box.

I waited in great anticipation. It never dawned on me that she would know it was me. I thought I was sneaky. Next thing you know, she grabbed my shirt collar and marched me straight to the principal's office. I'm sure Aunt LaLa "fell out laughin'" when she heard this one. But in true Aunt LaLa form, she paddled my behind anyway.

Note after note traveled from school to Mama and Aunt LaLa. You would think that I would have stopped bringing the notes home. Well, I am happy to say, even in my younger days, I was honest. Mostly.

I managed to figure out a solution. My reading wasn't getting any better, so I developed a new skill. You see, those notes from the teacher needed to be signed. My ingenious mind created my own carbon paper. Now you may not know what carbon paper is, but it worked like a charm.

I found a piece of paper and a soft-leaded pencil. I rubbed the paper so lead covered the entire sheet. Then, I hunted for something with Mama's signature. I traced Mama's signature with the lead-covered paper face down in the middle. It looked like Mama signed the note. I escaped a number of spankings with that technique.

Speaking of technique, aviators were working hard on their skills. They continued making great advancements. While I was in second grade (the first time), aviation engineers built the first all-metal monoplane fighter.

General Motors (Eastern) FM-1 Wildcat

Many things still amazed me. Clocks topped the list. I always wondered what made them tick. What made that sound? So, I took them apart. Every clock I could find, I tore it apart. Electricity still interested me. I continued to poke things in the sockets. Luckily, Mama was always able to talk the utility company out of turning off the electricity. Speaking of electricity, do you remember that Aunt LaLa was afraid of the dark?

Aunt LaLa sent me in the house first if it was dark out. I got tired of feeling around the house at night when the lights were off, so I rigged up a string. The string started from the light socket in the center of the room. It was on the ceiling. I tied the string from the socket to a nail that I pounded in the wall. It was next to the door.

One night I declared, "I'm not afraid of the dark."

I marched in the house and straight into bed. I left Aunt LaLa outside, too afraid of the dark to enter the house.

She hollered, "Franklin, you get out here!"

I just went to sleep.

Yes, I got it for that, too. That's why I rigged the string next to the door. Aunt LaLa could just reach in and pull on the lights. We both thought it was a great idea.

Frank and Aunt LaLa

School, on the other hand, was not so remarkable. Except Miss Karrison's room. I snuck out of my class to see what her class was doing. I wasn't interested because she was pretty. She allowed her students to do experiments. They made telephones with oatmeal boxes and string. (I put the instructions in the back of the book, in the appendix.) They built things like speakers. Thanks to General Palmer, science was a priority for Bristol School's sixth grade class.

Oh, it was great! I couldn't wait to get to her sixth grade class. Her room even had *Popular Mechanics* and *Popular Science* magazines.

Just look at those planes! Those magazines made me **_want_** to read.

I hid in the back of Mrs. Karrison's class.

One day she walked up to me and said, "Franklin, would you like to know what it says under those pictures?" Everyone knew I couldn't read. That was the day I decided I needed to figure it out.

Popular Science magazine

I can tell you it was not easy, but I had to learn. It took a lot of work. It caused me great frustration. So, I had to find something fun to do, like playing with carbide.

Now, the neighborhood we lived in was occupied by a lot of miners. Some of them were hard rock miners. Some were soft rock miners. The hard rock miners worked the gold mines up by Cripple Creek. The soft rock miners worked the coal mines north of town. They argued all the time about who were "real" miners.

Because of all the miners, Benton's Grocery down on the corner carried mining supplies. On the shelves sat mining lamps, batteries, caps, wiring, and things like this. I don't remember if they had dynamite, but they did carry calcium carbide. I still have a jar. The carbide burned in the miners' lamps to give them light. You put water in the container, and it would make acetylene gas. The

Frank's jar of carbide from childhood

gas was quite dangerous. That's why the miners sent canaries down the mine shaft. If that canary turned up its toes, the miners knew explosive fumes were present. The open flame from the candle lamps would cause an explosion. Carbide was everywhere. Old automobiles had carbide headlights. Miners wore carbide lights on their helmets. It sat on the shelf at the grocery store. Needless to say, kids bought carbide with the pennies they earned.

We took an Ovaltine can, drilled a hole in the bottom, put in some carbide, and put the friction top back on—but not too tight! Buster, Brother, and I spat in the can to get those gases going. The best part was when we took a match to it. The flame flashed in there and blew the cap off.

It was better than firecrackers. Boom! Bam! We placed our foot on the can so the lid traveled far. It was sort of a contest. Oh man, it made a tremendous noise. Today, I wouldn't do it because I'd be afraid I'd blow my foot off. You don't think of that when you're seven.

As Aunt LaLa would say, "Boy, I been further around the rim of the cup. Farther than you've been around the handle." It took some time, but I finally figured that old saying out. It meant Aunt

LaLa possessed wisdom. I did not. I have wisdom today, but I sure didn't at age seven. That's why I'm sharing with you. There's a lot of stuff we don't know when we are young. Like, how you might blow your foot off.

Ovaltine can

Chapter 6

Ol´ Man Loper and City Life

The basics. We used to call 'em the three R's: Reading, 'Riting, and 'Rithmetic. You should learn them! After you learn them, go find something that fascinates you. For me it was flight and mechanics. For you it might be music and cooking. Whatever it may be, give yourself an advantage. Learn the basics so you can acquire a skill.

The basics you learn in school are what help you achieve in an area that interests you when you get older. Some of the experiments you do at home help, too.

I thought, "Who needs all of that stuff?" when I was young.

Well, I was wrong when I was young. Now I know you need those basics.

I have always said, "School learns you how to learn." That means you go to school to learn how to learn. When you get older, you start to learn specific skills.

Get the basics. Gain a skill. Then go out there and get experience. Eventually your experience makes you an expert. It

Frank pretending to read

will also make you proud. Now back to my story.

Mama, Aunt LaLa, and I traveled out to San Francisco again. We went to San Francisco for Mama to marry Frank Loper. I called him Ol' Man Loper. He was great! I finally had a father figure.

Now, don't get me wrong. I still got my eight-year-old self into trouble.

We had just moved to San Francisco. At the time, I thought I was headed to third grade. Well, that wasn't happening. Mama and Aunt LaLa put me back in the second grade. This made me very upset.

Many years later, I learned Mama and Aunt LaLa put me back in second grade because I couldn't read. At the age of eight, I thought it was because the school was different, and they taught different stuff than the school in Colorado. Oh, I'm sure there were some topics that were different, but the reading, math, and spelling were the ***same*** . . . ***confusing!***

I decided I would learn to read, but it just doesn't happen that easily. My eyes weren't helping me, so I continued to use my ears. I listened to every word. That's how I passed some of my tests. Tests were very hard. I went over and over them. If my exams had a few pictures or diagrams, I answered correctly. If the test contained all words, there was trouble!

Each night when all was quiet, I went through everything I heard that day in my mind. I analyzed what the teacher said. I repeated it over and over in my brain. That's how my memory became so good. Ol' Man Loper taught me to do this as well.

I considered every question over and over. I could come up with a bunch of possible answers for every question. I even did this with math.

Frank acting like he is not in trouble

In San Francisco, I was mischievous. I was confused and bored. That's what got me in trouble. Well, so did my cousin Ruth. Ruth was a menace. She moved to San Francisco, too. She helped me get in trouble.

Now Ruth, she was just a flat-out nuisance. She'd be right in there with the boys. If we told her she couldn't play with us, she squealed, "I'm gonna tell Aunt Maude," and went straight over to Mama.

Ruth never got in trouble, but she should have.

Let me tell you, her only goal in life was to snitch on me.

In San Francisco, Ruth and I lived in the same apartment building. I lived on the bottom level. Ruth and her mother lived on the top floor. We spent many days pushing the elevator buttons. I stood in the lobby and pushed the button up. Ruth stayed upstairs and pushed the button for the elevator down. We had a lot of fun

Cousin Ruth and her father before he passed away

with that. Let me rephrase that. I got in trouble.

Ruth slid down the drain pipe to get to our apartment. She taught me to roller skate, too. I'm not so certain the streets of San Francisco were the best spot to learn roller skating, but that's what we did. Ruth found these old skates. They clamped onto your shoes. The nut fell off, so we used string to keep the wheels on the skate.

I learned the hard way that using string for a nut wasn't the best idea we ever had. Oh man, by the time I got to the bottom of the hill, I was skatin' alright. Skating and falling all at the same time. That string wore right away, and the back wheel came right off. I lasted about 3.6 seconds on three wheels, and then *splat!* Ruth went running. Not to help me, but straight to Mama.

"Franklin, I'm telling Aunt Maude."

And so it went. She came up with something, and I got in trouble.

Repeating second grade was rotten. You know I didn't like school to begin with. Now I had to go an extra year. I think I even blocked it out of my mind. I don't remember much about that school in San Francisco, but I do recall our walk to school.

It was the funniest thing. I thought those city kids were the dumbest kids in the world. You have to remember Colorado Springs was a ranching and mining community when I was a kid. I think the city had about 30,000 people. San Francisco was huge to us. San Francisco's population was well over 500,000.

When school started, I strolled from our place down to the school. On the way, all the neighborhood kids passed a dairy. We looked in the windows and watched the conveyer belt. It carried hundreds of glass bottles. Each bottle stopped just long enough to get filled with milk.

Ok, those kids we walked with were all from the city. They thought that milk came from the machine in the dairy. I told them that milk came from cows. The farmers just brought the milk in from the farm. They just laughed at me. Not a one of them believed me.

Well, I knew that I was right. Ol' Farmer Reed had cows back on Pine Street. We watched him milk the cows all the time. These city kids just didn't believe it.

The neighborhood kids did have fun. When we lived in San Francisco, they had what was called the Gilmore Fun Circus. It was a radio program that aired once a week. Remember, this was long before everyone had a television. It was 1931. The television had just been invented four years earlier in San Francisco.

The Gilmore Fun Circus had the Gilmore Lion. He was the mascot. The Gilmore radio show was bidding for the show to stay in San Francisco. Another company was trying to move the show to Los Angeles. They rounded up the neighborhood kids to be on the radio. They told us what to say and so on.

Gilmore Gas

Now, I thought this was great! I never cared about being a radio star. I was just interested in how they created all the sound effects. Coconut halves clopped like horses trotting. A thin sheet of metal waved in the air sounded like thunder. You should try it. We figured out all kinds of sound effects.

Sadly, San Francisco lost the contract.

That's not the only thing that got lost. Aunt LaLa got lost all the time. Oh, I remember this one day I walked downtown with Aunt LaLa. She got lost, and I was with her. I would like to make it very clear: I was not lost. It was Aunt LaLa who was lost.

We were out there, walking down the main street. She cried because she didn't know what way to go.

I said, "Just go a couple blocks that way. We can catch the street car."

She said, "You don't know what you're talkin' about."

She found a policeman. She went up to the officer, boo hooing.

Aunt LaLa said, "Sir, I just don't know how to find the street car to get home."

He said, "Well, ma'am, just go a couple of blocks down that way and get on the street car."

I said, "That's what I told her."

She said, "Shut up! Don't you talk back. I'll whip you right here."

I said, "The policeman won't let you."

She said, "I'll whip him, too."

Aunt LaLa was fumin'. I was right, you know. That made her mad.

That poor policeman knew he'd better side with Aunt LaLa, or she might just whip us both.

Around this same time and not too far from us in San Francisco, another great achievement in aviation history took place. Do you remember me telling you about Bessie Coleman? Do you remember me telling you William Powell opened that school? On Labor Day 1931 while we were in San Francisco, the Bessie Coleman Club made history. The first air show featuring all Black aviators performed in front of 15,000 spectators. Oh man, I wish I could have seen it. I probably would have jumped in one of the airplanes. After all, I flew with the Warden girls and their pilot boyfriends up at Alexander Aircraft.

This was around the same time Johnny Robinson and Cornelius Coffey traded an old Hudson car and $200 for a mere four hours of flight lessons and a Hummingbird Bi-plane. They were famous aviators of the time. Eventually both entered mechanics school. By the time they graduated from the master mechanics school, they were so good the director opened the school to all Black students.

The main reason we moved to San Francisco was for Mama to marry Frank Loper. He was the closest thing I ever knew to a father. Frank Loper originally lived most of the year in Colorado Springs. He came to the area with Jefferson Davis's daughter's family.

Frank Loper worked the hotels. That meant he had to move with tourist season. When tourism slowed down in Colorado Springs in the winter, Ol' Man Loper headed to California for work. I guess the original plan was to stay in San Francisco, but that all changed.

I never knew someone as proud or as proper as Frank Loper. He was born a slave on Jefferson Davis's plantation. Jefferson Davis was the President of the Confederate States during the Civil War. It was Jefferson Davis's daughter who brought Ol' Man Loper to Colorado a free man. They remained family friends for the rest of Frank Loper's life. Frank Loper was what you call a self-made man. Ol' Man Loper was so proper he creased his overalls. That means he ironed his work pants. He told me, "Franklin, you always need to look good."

He learned a lot from listening, too. You see, he worked the fancy hotels. He opened doors and carried luggage. Stuff like that. His personality was contagious. He never forgot a face or a name. Everyone loved hearing Ol' Man Loper's stories.

He listened in on all the talk. Those business men chatted up a storm in those hotel lobbies. He gathered information from San Francisco to Colorado Springs. He studied the markets just like those wealthy business men. He asked them questions. They told him the answers. In later years, he marched me right down to the Mining Exchange building and put his money into gold, steel, oil, and trains. He also loved real estate.

Frank Loper started a newspaper in Colorado Springs called *The Sun*. He told me to read between the lines. He helped found the People's Methodist Episcopal Church in Colorado Springs.

He worked at the Colorado Springs Fine Arts Center downtown. Even today, they have a giant painting of Ol' Man Loper in black tie and tails. It is on display during different times of year.

He was strictly Republican to start, he used to say. Every slave turned free man would have stayed Republican had they found work, but they didn't. The Emancipation Proclamation, after all, was from Lincoln, who was a Republican. He would say, "The Republican party left the emancipated slaves. They freed 'em but didn't teach them." In later years, I understood that to mean they should have trained them in the ideas of getting an education, work ethic, and accomplishment. He wasn't happy with the Democrats, either. He knew they figured out how to give people stuff. He didn't like that, so he became an Independent. Now, I'm not telling any of this for any other reason than an understanding of Ol' Man Loper. He prided himself on making something of himself. He never took a handout, but he always gave a helping hand to someone in need. He was a free man. That's the way it was going to stay. He was not going to owe anyone anything. It's just who he was.

Fortunately for me, he loved me like I was his own son. He taught me to be resilient. He showed me the value of hard work. He challenged me to do my best even when I thought my brain didn't work right. I was in second grade for the second time, but Ol' Man Loper never questioned my abilities. As a matter of fact, he did not give me any slack.

After Mama married Ol' Man Loper, I felt very thankful. They were much older. I think Mama was in her late fifties. Aunt LaLa was at least eight years older. Ol' Man Loper was older than both of my aunts. He never knew his age, though. His records were burned during the Civil War.

Now don't think that kept me out of all the mischief. My curious mind was still at work, but Ol' Man Loper helped me use that curiosity in useful ways. He would say, "Only believe half of what you see and nothing that you hear. Go figure it out for yourself."

One day Mama and Aunt LaLa were all worked up because they couldn't find me. They thought I was missing. Aunt LaLa always got lost, so naturally she believed I was out wandering, alone somewhere in the city. Well, I knew right where I was. I was in the basement of the Bellevue Hotel. I had followed Ol' Man Loper to work that day. He had a dressing room in the basement. The interesting thing to me was not the dressing room, but how we got down there. The Bellevue Hotel had moving stairs. Today we would say "an escalator."

I spent hours under those moving stairs. They were just mesmerizing to me. I grabbed one of Ol' Man Loper's chocolate snack cakes and laid right under those stairs. I watched them for hours. I tried to figure out how the whole thing worked. So, there I was, just covered in chocolate crumbs. Eventually Mama and Aunt LaLa came to tell Ol' Man Loper I was missing. He just laughed and pointed to the basement.

Shortly after that little episode, I am thankful to say, we headed back to Colorado Springs for good. After all, Pine Street was always my favorite.

CHAPTER 7

Water Tank Rockets and Mumbley Peg

We stayed in San Francisco for eighteen months. I never liked it much, except for the museum. I was fascinated by the Egyptian displays. I dreamed of living in those ancient times. I especially liked the scarabs.

We had some fun in San Francisco, but I missed Brother and Buster down on Pine Street. Pine Street was home.

I was thrilled when we moved back.

When we moved back from San Francisco, one of the people who missed me most was my friend Grace. She was afraid she would never see me again. When I was eight and Grace was ten, we decided we should get married. We figured her dad would marry us. He was a reverend. He kindly refused. He said she was too old for me. It made me mad. To this day, we joke about that.

I thought I would get to jump up to fourth grade with my friends. Remember, they completed third grade while I was out in San Francisco. As you all know, that's not how it works. It disturbed me. I went straight to third grade. My friends? They were all in fourth grade. They hadn't flunked like I had.

At school, I continued to sneak out of my class to see what the sixth grade class was doing just like I did when I was in second grade. Miss Karrison still allowed her students to make telephones out of oatmeal boxes and everything. I thought that was just great. I couldn't read, but my science skills started falling into place. I really had a knack for it.

I passed the age of dipping girls' pigtails in ink wells, but I replaced it with putting carbide in ink wells.

Now Buster and Brother and I always had a little something going on at school or in the neighborhood. We worked hard at mastering all of carbide's options. Today, people would make a law against it or something. Probably call the police on you for messing with it. Back then, it was normal kid stuff. We just put our imaginations together to have a little fun. Eventually Buster and Brother started playing sports. We stayed good friends, but we didn't play as much. I thought sports were ok, but I really enjoyed mechanical things. So, I kept hanging out at the Wardens' house. They had a garage full of mechanical tools, Model T's, and so forth. It was a nine-year-old boy's heaven.

Then life got even better. Around this time, the Saunders moved in and became our other neighbors. They had three boys. It was terrific!

Bobby Saunders and I were two peas in a pod, as they used to say. He loved mechanical things as much as me. Most of the neighborhood, like Brother and Buster, continued with their sports. Not us. We were "innovators."

That reminds me of one of our all-time best neighborhood creations. The Carbide Propelled Water Tank Rocket. Naturally, I was the test pilot.

We had one of those hot water tanks that sat next to the stove. That's how families got hot water back then. The wood burning stove heated the water in the tank that was attached. The hot water ran to the sink, or it was piped to the bathroom for a hot bath. I guess you could say it was the first hot water heater.

Aunt LaLa, Mama, and guest in front of the water tank, which was later to be used as Frank and Bobby Saunder's rocket

Anyway, the tank in our house was new. It wasn't rusted out.

The tank we were interested in was the old rusted one in the backyard. Ol' Man Loper put that corroded old contraption out back. It sat and sat. The Saunders boys and I decided it had a better use. You know, back then, everything had a use.

We took it out front on Pine Street. Bobby turned the tank on its side and strapped it to our wagon. It might have been a chug. Whatever it was, it had wheels. We placed a bunch of carbide in the open hole at the top. That hole was at the rear of our rocket. We sealed it right up so the gases would collect inside the tank. The idea was for the flames to propel that rocket right down Pine Street.

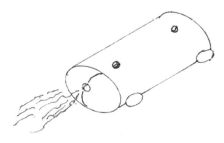

Frank's drawing of the Pine Street
water tank rocket

We aimed that tank down the street. Of course, I rode the thing. Pine Street had a slope to it, so the rocket rolled a little. That was not good enough. We had visions of going to space. We wanted to shout, "Blast off!"

We crammed more carbide in the top hole where the tube used to be attached. We added a few more lumps. Next step, we poured a little water to activate it. Then, Bobby took a long stick and lit the gases as it came out of the rear of the tank.

We thought it would go down the street like a rocket.

Next thing I knew, flames shot out of the back like a blow torch.

Flames flew out the back, but no lift off. Then the Saunders grabbed the sides and ran me down the road. Thrust had nothing to do with it. From a scientific point of view, it was a great failure. No rocket propulsion. From a reaction standpoint, it was fabulous.

I piloted that rocket right down the street. Flames shootin' behind. Old Man Benton from the grocery store stood in a panic. Our rocket was the biggest blow torch you ever saw. He thought I was going to blow up his gas tanks that stood by the curb. I stopped right in front of his store. Oh man, he fumed! His face turned purple.

By the time I made it back up the hill to our house, Old Man Benton had called Mama.

He shouted something to the effect of, "I will never sell carbide to those no good boys again."

Now, remember, we had one of the four telephones in the neighborhood. Everyone knew our phone number. It took seconds for Ol' Man Benton to call Mama. That rocket program came to a screeching halt. Another failed "great" idea.

It all led to another trip to the piano bench for Franklin. I sang many spirituals that day to "straighten me out." That event may have required both singin' and a trip to the switch bush. I can't remember.

That experience taught me that I had a real knack for science. After all, that rocket "almost" worked. If you would like to know why it did not work as planned, you can investigate rocket propulsion. Take a balloon, blow it up, and let it go. Where is the pressure that makes it fly forward? I'll give you a clue. It's not the air coming out of the back of the balloon. That was a question I had to answer later when I took my test to enter flight school.

When I listened to *Buck Rogers and the Twenty-Fifth Century* on the radio, it sparked my imagination. I could only imagine the things I could do—flying being the most important.

We were brilliant back then, but we didn't know anything. We were just lucky the good Lord looked after us day after day. If those flames burned inside the tank of our rocket, I would have launched for real. That tank would have blown up and sent me straight to the hospital or worse.

When I think of all these things I did as a child, I remember Mama saying, "The good Lord looks after babies and drunks and young boys." Mama added young boys on my account.

By this time, I had figured out one trick with my reading. I started using my fingers to keep the letters and words from getting all muddled. That means "mixed up." I took my pointer finger of my left hand. I placed it on the line below the line I needed to read. At the same time, I used my right-hand pointer finger to follow along each word. When I stopped at the first line, I looked for my left-hand pointer finger. It showed me right where my eyes had to go to read the next line. I touched my right pointer finger to my left. Then I slid my left pointer down to the next line. I did this for the entire book. It started to help a little.

I still struggled, though. I sat in the back of the classroom every chance I got. Partly to hide from the teacher and partly to practice my reading. I practiced reading the captions of the *Popular Mechanics* magazines. This helped me because I understood the pictures.

I decoded the words that would match the pictures. If you have a hard time reading, you can do what I did. Find magazines about things you like. If you enjoy food and cooking, read cooking magazines. If you prefer mechanical things like me, *Popular Science* is still published. I will also tell you there are many people who will help you. You have to decide to let them help. Also, you must practice. That's how you get better at doing something.

Now, Ol' Man Loper knew I had a hard time reading, but he realized I loved taking things apart. He surprised me on my birthday with a Mickey Mouse pocket watch. Oh man, I had always wanted that pocket watch.

When he came home one day, that pocket watch was in various states of disassembly, pieces spread all over the dining room table.

Mama said, "Oh, Dad's gonna get on you. Oh, you shouldna' done it."

Ol' Man Loper came home from work, walked right by me, and said, "Looks like you're enjoying that watch, son."

So Ol' Man Loper was in trouble with Mama. She fussed at him.

He said, "Well, I knew he was going to tear it up. He tears everything else up."

I loved tearing stuff up. Not ripping it apart, but taking it apart to see how it worked. That's why I couldn't wait for the sixth grade, Mrs. Karrison's class.

One day Mrs. Karrison took the sections out of an orange crate. She cut a round hole in there. The students took a bladder or lung of some animal, and Mrs. Karrison set a weight on it. The weight helped the skin dry in the correct shape. When the bladder dried, the students put a string through it. They made a speaker. It was great. We could talk through it. It magnified sound and everything.

At this point, Mama was still making me say, "Every day and in every way, I'm getting better and better." Like before, Aunt JuJu still called Mama to tell on me when I yelled down the street, "In every day and every way, I'm getting worser and worser."

Mama dressed me to the nines. That means "fancy." She and Ol' Man Loper took pride in looking good. I wore these short pants to school. I had to wear long socks. I got past Aunt JuJu's, and I rolled those things right down to my ankles.

Aunt JuJu marched back to Mama's.

"Maudella, I don't know why you put those stockin's on that boy. He rolls 'em down the second he walks around the corner."

Franklin J. Macon with his unwanted long stockings

No self-respecting nine-year-old wants to wear those at school.

When we returned to Pine Street, Grandpa Warden and Ol' Man Loper hit it right off. They went out in the backyard and practiced their trick shooting. They were great shots. Grandpa Warden set cans on the fence. One by one he shot them right off the rail . . . Ping! Ping! Ping! The rest of us never knew, but they used old fake bullets to do those tricks. I never took to shooting because I couldn't hit a thing. I had an astigmatism. That means I have oddly-shaped eyes. It meant I couldn't line up my actions with my eyes like other kids. Aiming at a basket or hitting a ball? Oh man, I was terrible.

Ol' Man Loper bought me a basketball and hoop. I was athletic, but I was terrible at sports that required aiming. Basketball? Just forget it. He put that hoop up there on the house. If that net had been as big as our house and I had a beach ball, I still missed that hoop. Same with baseball. If I ever did hit it, it was gone.

Now don't get me wrong. I was very coordinated. I tumbled on the gymnastics team when I was older. I just didn't have good hand-eye coordination. My eyes are still bad. Probably another reason I struggled to read.

You ask, "How did I manage to fly?" Well, the local eye doctor told me, years later, to memorize the eye chart. He taught me a few other tricks, too. I think he wanted me to fly almost as much as I wanted to fly. I passed that eye test with flying colors.

Back then, many gutsy aviators just wanted to fly. Thomas C. Allen was just like me. He worked odd jobs around the airfields just to get in the air. One day he hopped in a plane and soloed without permission. He didn't care. He soared in the air. Eventually Allen became one of the famous Flying Hobos.

The Famous Flying Hobos

The other aviator's name was J. Herman Banning. They were extraordinary aviators. They flew an old World War I Eagle Rock bi-plane across the country. Someone had offered them $1,000 to accomplish the feat. They certainly made it. The trip took two weeks.

They never found the sponsor to pay, but they made a name for themselves.

Banning had all kinds of aviation adventures. What I like best was he built his own plane.

Back in Colorado Springs, I was having my own adventures. I remember Frank Loper bought me a BB gun while I was in third grade. He probably thought I might take to shooting like he and Grandpa Warden. Of course, I took it to school. Now you probably thought I got in trouble for that. Nope! The teacher said to leave it by her desk until recess, so I did. Today you **cannot ever** take such things to school, but back then, it was normal.

We got out and shot at anything we could during recess. Not each other, of course. We knew better. We aimed at trees, the fence, and squirrels. Stuff like that. I brought that BB gun home at lunch just as my teacher said, and that was the end of that. Today you can hardly have a sharp pencil at school. That's how things have changed over the years.

Back then, every boy had to have the best Boy Scout pocket knife, too. If you didn't, the other boys thought there was something wrong with you. We played Mumbley Peg. The object of the game was to take your pocket knives and flip 'em up in the air to hit a target on the ground. I liked the game ok, but I would rather tear up a clock or radio.

Today adults would panic if they saw such a game. Back then, no one got hurt and adults paid no attention. We all knew, if we weren't responsible, a parent would snatch that item away and you'd never get it back. ***Ever!***

Also, for the second time in my life, we had a dog. Ol' Man Loper had this old police dog named Blanyo.

This is how they named him: There was a missionary from Africa at our church. They asked this lady what "dog" was in Swahili or something like that.

She said, "Blanyo." From that day on, the dog was named Blanyo.

I figured out how to handle Aunt LaLa's old chickens. It took me a couple of years, but I solved my problem. I sent Blanyo right into the chicken house. Blanyo ran after those birds like it was the best day of his life. Once Blanyo got the chickens cornered, I blocked them in with the big plywood board. It kept those birds from pecking at me while I cleaned.

This dog followed Ol' Man Loper everywhere. Ol' Man Loper rode his bike all over town. Blanyo ran right behind. I tell you this because Ol' Man Loper never learned how to drive. He started out way too late in life. He just lacked coordination. Remember there was no such thing as automatic transmission in the 1930's. The Wardens taught me to drive their Model A around the time I was six years old. It's no wonder playing with clothespin Pilgrims wasn't so exciting for me back in kindergarten.

Frank's nickel pony ride

Another one of the fun things we would do was hook our police dog to the wagon. We had an old wind-up Victrola. That's a record player . . . if you know what that is.

We placed that Victrola right in the wagon. Blanyo pulled the wagon up and down the street. We wound up the Victrola and played the records. We sang the songs. We didn't always notice the needle bounced all around. It jumped right off the record and made scratches all over the place, another not-too-successful neighborhood plan. Our folks were not pleased. They hollered about their scratched-up records. Oh well, we had a grand time singing through the neighborhood.

CHAPTER 8

Coal Truck and Chicken Coop

I was approaching the magic age of ten. As you know, young boys can dream up any number of things. That's exactly what Bobby Saunders and I did. We were inseparable. We just started doing things. Reuben and Ted, too. They were Bobby's younger brothers.

That's how we started digging a tunnel under the fence. There isn't a ten-year-old boy who wants to walk around to the front of the house when you can dig a perfectly good tunnel under the yard fence. That passageway worked perfectly during the summer. Bobby and I crawled under that fence every day. We went from our house to the Saunders ten times a day just to go under the fence.

We decided to dig a huge hole in the middle of the yard, too. After all, Ol' Man Loper dug a big hole to make a coal bin. Back then, everyone heated their homes by burning coal. To store the coal, a big hole was dug somewhere in the yard. It was sort of like a cellar. We figured Mama and Mrs. Saunders would think it was a terrific option for our club house.

Now Ol' Man Loper's hole was next to the house for the coal storage. He cemented the walls and covered the giant gap in the ground. Bobby and I shoveled our hole right in the middle of the backyard.

Winter arrived. The snow fell and covered our hole. We never thought anything about it. We covered it with two-by-fours and corrugated tin. We put dirt right over the top so no one could see it.

One afternoon, the big old coal truck drove to our house. It rounded the corner of the house and headed to the backyard. He backed that big truck smack in the center of our hole. He had planned to park right along the coal cellar. He backed up, not expecting a thing. Next thing you know, he was stuck dead center in our hole. That truck went straight down. Trapped! No way was that loaded coal truck driving out.

The coal driver slammed his door. He carried five divisions in his truck loaded with coal. Mama had to buy each and every one of the five sections of coal. We usually bought one. On account of the truck getting stuck in the hole in our yard, the whole load was ours. Five dollars a ton. Oh, I was in deep yogurt that time. Back then, twenty-five dollars was a small fortune.

We walked down the street to Farmer Reed's. That's how we pulled that old coal truck out of our wonderful club house hole. We shoveled all five sections of coal into the coal bin. At about a ton a section, you can just imagine. It took us until dark to empty the truck. Once again, my inventive skills got me in trouble.

It was 1933. I was just getting started. Bobby and I drew up airplane models. We'd whittle them out of wood. You couldn't buy models like you can today. That's how we started making wings. It was the fourth grade. Far away in Chicago, people were showing each other all these new and brilliant ideas that would change the future of the world. I'm not sure who had more inventions, the Chicago World's Fair or Pine Street?

Brother and Buster weren't as excited about innovation; they were still out throwing a ball. You know, that was just fine. We all have different abilities and activities that interest us.

Bobby Saunders and I were ready for anything.

Goodwill Flight Poster

Kind of like Dr. Albert Forsythe and C. Alfred "Chief" Anderson. This same year, these two aviators proved to the world what they were made of.

They were the first African-Americans to fly coast-to-coast. Believe it or not, Chief taught himself how to fly. He saved enough money. He bought a secondhand plane. No one would teach him, so he just watched others and taught himself. I say, that's determination.

Mrs. Roosevelt and "Chief" Anderson on their famous flight at Moton Field

Chief later became famous for a 1941 flight. Oh, his first solo was sure something, but his flight with Mrs. Eleanor Roosevelt changed the world. She went home and said to the President, "Franklin, I flew with those boys down there [at Tuskegee], and you're going to have to do something about it."

While the country was getting ready to "do something about it," Bobby Saunders and I were doing something about our flying.

Back in those days, we had clothes lines. Everyone had these poles to prop up the line for the clothes to dry. The poles were made of bamboo.

Bobby and I thought, "We can use those for wings." They were real light, or so we thought. We covered them with burlap bags and canvas. We even used newspaper. To use newspaper, we made flour and water paste as glue. We carefully constructed our wings. Bobby strapped them on my arms with rope.

We were ready to fly. Bobby tied me into the wings. I didn't have the strength to move them. We adjusted. Instead of one wing on each arm, we made one giant wing. That way we used the strength of two arms for one long wing.

We ran down the street flapping our homemade wings. The neighbors thought, "Miss Macon's kid is just nuts!"

It never worked running down the street. So, we, in our genius ten-year-old minds, decided we needed a little help. First, we tied the wings to our bikes. Bobby peddled. We peddled like crazy.

Once again, no lift off.

That's when we had the brilliant idea of jumping off the chicken house. We hopped up there with our homemade wings. Up we went. We jumped straight off the top of the chicken coop.

I flapped and flapped. You guessed it. The aerodynamics were not great. Gravity. Now that old gravity worked like a charm.

The roof had a little slant. It was about seven or eight feet off the ground. Wasn't very high, but it was high enough. I took a running start.

Thankfully, the dirt on the backside of the chicken coop had been dug up for the garden. We figured out fast that that was the best place to land. We crashed with style.

Now you might be asking, "Did you ever get hurt?" Well, when you're young and limber, hitting the ground isn't all that bad. You knew you'd landed, but we always bounced back.

I always say that was my first "unsuccessful" solo.

I have no doubt I got in trouble for jumping off the chicken coop. I also have no doubt that Aunt LaLa laughed herself right out of her old rocking chair watching us.

As far as toys were concerned, I had a few favorites. Most I made. One was the scooter. We used roller skates for the wheels. We sometimes used orange crates. That is what that box is on the front of the scooter. If you want to make a scooter, I put some directions in the back of the

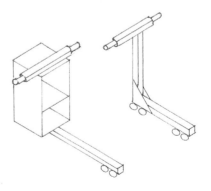

Frank's drawing of childhood scooters

book. Today, I think skateboard wheels would work just fine.

I also had a good-sized toy dump truck. I'm not sure what happened to that. Sometimes the Davis family would give me toys when their kids grew up. That was the family Frank Loper worked for. They were the ones who brought him to Colorado Springs after the Civil War. Remember, Ol' Man Loper was born on a slave plantation. Jefferson Hayes-Davis was the grandson of Jefferson Davis, President of the Confederacy. Jefferson Davis owned the plantation where Ol' Man Loper was born like I mentioned earlier. Jefferson Hayes-Davis was the Vice President of the First National Bank of Colorado Springs. He and Ol' Man Loper always remained close. They treated each other like family.

Now my cousins up the street had an electric train. It was beautiful. It had a fancy track. It had lights that went on and off. I got one that was not near as fancy. Just round pieces of track. No light. Nothing like that. I got tired of my cousin braggin', so I fixed the problem.

It was around Christmas time. I looked at our Christmas tree, all lit up, and I got an idea. I snipped off a couple of Christmas lights and hooked them to my train. To this day, I have no idea how I knew to fasten those lights up to the train, but I did.

I told my cousins, "I have lights on my train, and I did it myself."

Of course, the Christmas lights on the tree didn't work anymore, but those train lights worked just fine.

Mama worked for the Rudder family. Mr. Rudder got me a mechanical drawing set. Oh man, that was great. I was always drawing houses and plans for airplanes. I realized I was good at it. Later, I took mechanical drawing in junior high school. That's when things started to improve at school. My math skills were still awful, but I could draw a layout or schematic with little effort. I saw the picture in my mind and boom! I had it on paper.

Mr. Rudder bought me an Erector set. Then, he bought me a chemistry set. It was outstanding. It came in a wooden box. It had a book, but my friends and I never even read the instruction book. It was far more fun to make up our own chemical concoctions. The "bang" was always bigger!

I tried a bunch of the chemicals. They would bubble a little and so on. After a couple of experiments, I decided a little carbide was needed. Now, I know what you are thinking. Ol' Man Benton stopped selling carbide to us after the whole rocket incident. You're right. But we lived in a neighborhood full of miners. Carbide was everywhere. We could get it from the other neighborhood kids whose fathers worked in the mines.

I added carbide to everything in that chemistry set. I had things poppin' and bangin' all over the place. Later that year, we got into crystal sets. We were instructed, "No more rockets!" So, we decided on radios. We made our own crystal sets. If you think we just took some sugar and water and food coloring to create sugar crystals, you are wrong. Back in 1933, a crystal set meant you made your own radio receiver. Somehow we knew how this all worked. I guess we learned from the older kids.

If I recall, we ordered our crystals from Radio Shack or something. Back then, Radio Shack was for people who made their own radios. The crystals were only ten or fifteen cents.

The crystal went in the center. Today they are called "diodes." Back then, we used galena.

Inventions like this were exactly why I could not wait to get into Mrs. Karrison's class. She had experiments like that all the time. Bobby and I couldn't wait, so we made anything we could at home.

One day, I lost my crystal, so I hooked onto the Saunders boys' antenna. Bobby, Reuben, and Ted wired their set from the garage

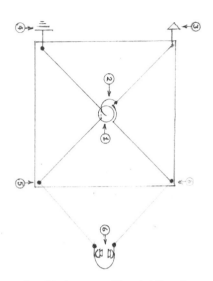

Frank's drawing of his childhood
crystal set radio

to the house, and from the house to the chicken shed. Ted hit just the right spot. Instead of a radio station, Ted heard our conversation through the headset. We were stunned. We thought we had invented a telephone.

Bobby and I had a great time with those old radios, but they still were not as fun as flying. That old flying bug never did leave me. I rode my bicycle up to Alexander Aircraft as often as I could. I was a real pest up there, always asking questions and so on. Finally, the Alexander Airplane Factory closed down, but the airstrip was still there. The Depression was going on, so people didn't spend money on things like airplanes. Then, I went out to the airport. I washed planes and swept the hangar. They'd take me flying for payment.

I learned a lot from those pilots up at Alexander, but I learned much, much more from Ol' Man Loper. He taught me to be meticulous. That means to give great care about the details.

Ol' Man Loper always made me take nails out of old wooden boards. He had me straighten those things right out. He was particular. I pounded and pounded. If each nail was not perfectly straight, I started over. We did this so often, I didn't even know you could go to the hardware store and buy brand new nails that were straight. I thought all nails came out of boards and everyone had to straighten 'em. When I did figure that out, I wondered why

Ol' Man Loper expected perfection. I realized it was not so much about the nails. It was about doing a job with great care. I think of that today. If I had not taken great care in fixing the aircrafts I worked on, pilots would not have been safe.

I am happy to say that I actually taught Ol' Man Loper something, too.

Ol' Man Loper could not drive. Horses, guns, bicycles. That was his life. But a car? He just couldn't manage it. One day, he decided he needed to learn. This is how the story goes.

There was a lady everyone called Cousin Neck. She was born on Jefferson Davis's plantation just like Frank Loper. Ol' Man Loper could not get along with her. No matter what he did, they just didn't get along. Now Mama would go visit Cousin Neck. Ol' Man Loper would never go in that house.

He would say, "I'm not going into Ol' Neckie's house!"

So, one day Ol' Man Loper decided I needed to teach him how to drive. That way he could drop Mama off to visit Cousin Neck, and Ol' Man Loper didn't have to sit and wait. After all, you never knew how long the visiting would go on. Those ladies could talk.

I thought, "I know how to drive." So, I decided it would be easy to teach Ol' Man Loper. I showed him how to push in the clutch and move the gears.

"Here's first, second, third, and reverse. You push in on that and bring it down. You push on the clutch to go to second." Back then, nothing was automatic.

Well, Ol' Man Loper started that car. He let off the clutch. Off went the car. Zoom, bang, boom! Across the dirt road, up the curb, over to the other side. He high centered that old Nash right on the dirt berm. We were stuck. He revved that engine. The wheels spun. The harder he tried to get free, the more stuck we got. Those old wheels were inches off the ground.

Ol' Man Loper and Mama had to go get their friend and his car to pull our car off the curb. If that hadn't worked, I'm sure Farmer Reed's horses would have done the trick. Lucky for me, the car worked.

Mama was upset. Not with Ol' Man Loper. She hollered at me. I got in trouble.

I still thought it was great because the folks in the neighborhood told Ol' Man Loper, "You should've let the kid drive."

I thought, "You got that right!"

Eventually Ol' Man Loper took me down to the police station. He asked if I could just drive for him. They said, "Yes."

I still couldn't read, at least not well, but I sure could drive. After all, I was ten.

CHAPTER 9

Crackin' the Wall and Jumpin' the Bridge

In fifth grade, I got more information out of a drawing than reading a paragraph about any subject.

It was 1934. The Dust Bowl caused by severe droughts crippled the country. I hated reading, and I learned I loved science and mechanics. Those were exciting! Somehow I understood how to figure torque and gear ratios. I couldn't add, subtract, multiply, or divide more than two numbers in a row, but I could build about anything.

Science interested me so much I created my own experiments. I used my brain like Ol' Man Loper told me. It probably wasn't what he had in mind, but it sure worked for me.

For me, using my brain meant thinking to myself, "Sneak some carbide to school." This is something I suggest you **_not_** do.

I snuck into my classroom. I plopped carbide right into the ink well of a couple of desks. The stuff created a gas. It bubbled the ink right out and onto the desk. Oh, it was a mess! And that smell! It was worse than sulfur. You would never forget that odor if you smelled that carbide.

My plan worked, though. I didn't have to take that day's quiz because the pen ink had bubbled all over the desks. At the age of eleven, I thought that was a brilliant way to use my brain. Until I got home. Bad idea. Now that I think of it, that was probably one of those times when a note was sent home by the teacher. Actually, I think that one was a phone call to my house. Of course, it ended with another spankin'.

Speaking of spankin's, there was a gal who took care of me. I can't remember her name. It wasn't Hazel or Erma, the Warden girls. It was another neighborhood girl. When she was over at our house, she spent her time listening to the radio shows. I don't think she had a radio at her house. She made phone calls, too. Basically, she didn't watch me at all.

Of course, this did not bother me one bit. The bad part? She made me stay in the house. I didn't care for that so much, so I got creative.

I liked to take these old dining room chairs, line 'em up, and take an old Army blanket to make a fort. I crawled up underneath. I always made a lot of noise. I had done this every time she was over until this one day.

I got bored with my fort-making, so I made an engineering decision.

At this time, Mama's friends would give me old spools and snuff cans. You know, the old wooden ones. I used them for all kinds of things. I made what we called "tractors." You take a spool with a match stick and a button for a bearing. String it up with a rubber band. Wind it up, and off it goes. Your own homemade tractor.

I put some directions at the end of the book if you want to make one.

On this particular day, I didn't just want to use the spools for toy tractors. I was bored with my fort, so I made a new project. Believe it or not, this helped me with a main test I had to

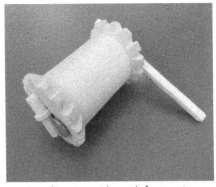

Spool tractor with teeth for traction

take at Keesler Field. That's the test I passed to go to flight school at Tuskegee.

I made all kinds of noise as usual. The babysitter never paid it any mind. She thought I was building another fort. She was wrong!

In those days, we had plaster walls. Once in a while these things cracked. If it cracked, people covered the wall with fancy floral wallpaper.

Well, the kitchen had this plaster.

I thought, "I have a brilliant idea."

I nailed those spools all along the wall. Then, I hooked strings around all the spools to lift different weights.

I attached different weights to figure out gear ratios and so on. I also made a small model.

You could try this at home without getting in trouble for cracking the wall.

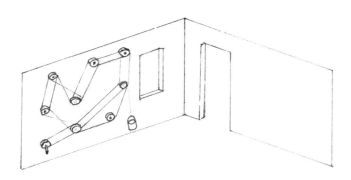

Frank's drawing of "Crackin' the Wall"

Now this was all going along just fine. I switched the strings to move different gears. I tried different items for weights. I figured out gear ratios for the different-sized spools. I was having a wonderfully inventive time until . . .

I wrecked the wall. It was full of **_big_** cracks! I split the wall in several spots. Every nail I hit caused a crack.

Mama came home. Once again, she did not think too highly of my mechanical achievements.

I know she wanted to whip me, but that was usually up to dear Aunt LaLa. I think she had a paddle in every corner of the house.

Mama hollered at that poor babysitter.

Mama went right in there, "Didn't you hear him out there bangin' on the wall?"

The babysitter said, "He's always beatin' on something. I figured if I heard him, I knew where he was."

Mama, like I mentioned earlier, wasn't too good at whippin's. She talked me to death first, followed by the singin'.

I sang to "save" my soul. I'm just thankful I am around today to tell you the story. I never saw Mama so mad in my life. Today, I just laugh about it.

When I'd see this girl in later years, I'd just fall out laughin'. I think she got in more trouble than me. Now, I don't want you to get in trouble like I did. That's why I made a small version. The instructions are in the appendix.

Fifth grade continued. I conducted my own experiments. I failed at most of my reading and math, but I tried. Oh boy, did I try. I never gave up, which I am happy to say is a trait of many of my fellow aviators. Just as I was struggling with my math lessons, Willa

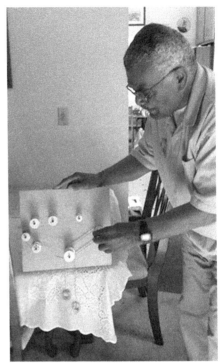

Frank demonstrating the gear ratios from his childhood experiment

Brown, another great aviatrix, started taking flying lessons.

Originally, Willa Brown was a teacher and social worker. I guess she wanted a little more adventure. In 1934, she decided to take flying lessons. A few years later, she became the first female Black commercial pilot. She didn't stop there. She eventually started a flight school and became the first female Black officer in the Civil Air Patrol.

Willa Brown

Now in fifth grade, I had no idea that Willa Brown took flying lessons. I really didn't know about the Civil Air Patrol. It didn't exist yet. But you know what? It had an impact on my life. I never dreamed that one day the Civil Air Patrol in Colorado Springs would be where I'd take my first successful solo flight.

Being eleven years old, I really didn't pay attention to much outside of our neighborhood, unless it had something to do with flying. Back in the neighborhood, I did know a few things. I did know Reverend Morgan had thirteen kids. There were three girls around our age. This was great. Not because they were cute. Because they screamed louder than anyone in a five-block radius.

Brother, Buster, and I still liked to pull a few tricks.

Up the street lived the Leaf family. They were the ones who did the concrete work. They had some old machines and old water tanks in their yard. They chained these tanks together instead of using a fence. Well, the Morgan girls would go to church. When they walked back at night, we hid behind those tanks. We put sheets over our heads. We scared them like we were ghosts. We jumped out and terrified them.

They could run faster and scream louder than anything. It was great fun!

Now, I was still trying my best at school. My tries usually ended up in disaster, but Ol' Man Loper, Mama, and Aunt LaLa kept encouraging me. I can't tell you how many times I was sent home. Of course, I usually didn't make it straight home. I walked up to the clay banks. I found a perfect spot, laid on the ground, and watched the sky. I studied the cloud formations. More importantly, I pondered a lot of questions. Do you ever do that?

Some questions I found answers to over the years, and some I am still in wonder over today at the age of ninety-four. Here are some of my favorites:

1. What keeps the Earth spinning at the same speed all the time?
2. What is night time, and where does it go when the sun comes up?
3. Has the sun always come up in the East?
4. Where did the sun, moon, and stars come from?
5. Why can't you see the stars in the daytime?
6. What makes the stars twinkle? Is there a big light switch that turns them on every night?
7. Why does everyone have a real mother and dad and brothers and sisters, and I don't?
8. Who is my real mother and dad? Why am I with Mama and LaLa?

9. Why does dirt turn into mud when it is wet, and sand just gets wet?
10. How do baby chicks get into an egg?
11. What makes fire hot?
12. Why does it snow when it is winter and rain when it is summer?
13. What makes the wind blow?
14. Why do I have trouble reading and doing math?
15. Where do people come from, and why do they all look different?
16. Why do I have to go to school? It's no fun!
17. What makes that ticking sound in a clock?
18. How do they make the stuff that makes the lights work?

Stuff like that.

Now, clouds were a mystery to me. Water, too. I even wondered how the water would get outside the glass in the summer. You see, in 1934, I had no understanding of condensation and things like this.

I didn't understand, but that wasn't an excuse to quit. So, I didn't quit, and I found out the answer.

I'm happy to say that not all days at school were bad. Matter of fact, the more I tried, the better it got.

I even got treats when I got home with no note from the teacher.

If I didn't get a beating at school all day, Mama baked my favorite food. Oh, by the way, the whippin's and beatin's from Aunt LaLa didn't hurt a bit, but I put on a great crying show. Then I ran outside and laughed about it. It did get my attention that I messed up. I tried not to get caught again.

Back to Mama's food. I liked Indian rice and round steak and lemon pie with graham cracker crust. I had to take the rollin' pin to make the graham cracker crust for the lemon pie, but it was worth the work. Once in a great while, maybe because I only had twenty whippin's instead of twenty-five, I earned that favorite meal. Mama knew just how to prepare it.

Ol' Man Loper loved rice. Mama would make up more rice on Fridays than what we were going to eat for dinner. She would keep the rice and mix it into the pancake dough for Sunday. Ol' Man Loper and I thought we were living in tall cotton when Mama made her rice pancakes. The maple came in a block back then. It was a whole dollar. You made it into syrup. That was a treat. Mama heated it and mixed in brown sugar.

Ol' Man Loper liked rice, and he loved honey, too. The ol' man had some bees down at the other end of the yard. I learned fast, so they never bothered me. They crawled on me. Never got stung.

Once in a while, those bees helped me outsmart Aunt LaLa when she was going to whip me. I would run out back by the beehives. Those old bees would not sting me, but they would tear Aunt LaLa up. They were my protectors along with my dog, Boots. Later in the day, I would forget Aunt LaLa was going to spank me and go back in the house. Oh boy, would she get me then. No bees in the house.

I never was a hero-worshipper. That means I didn't love the people in the movies or on the radio like some of my friends did. Well, I loved Buck Rogers, but I really admired real people who accomplished stuff. That's another reason I loved my Ol' Man Loper. He was loved all around Colorado Springs.

I also looked up to people who were innovators. I couldn't care less if someone was famous in Hollywood. I admired people who worked hard.

That reminds me, I need to tell you about Benjamin O. Davis Jr. While I was trying my best to get from fifth grade to sixth grade, he toiled his way through the Military Academy at West Point. He was the first Black man to earn his commission at West Point. I thought school was hard for me. I don't think General Davis ever had trouble with reading or math, but he wasn't treated too kindly. Not a soul talked to him while he was at the Academy. I'm here to tell you, he did not give up, either. Today he is one of the most famous Air Force Generals. He even commanded the Ninety-ninth Fighter Squadron out of Tuskegee.

It just goes to show you, you can't give up.

Now back to the neighborhood. Just like when we were little, we loved to sing: the old cowboy songs and the latest tunes. We knew them all. The Saunders boys and I sang at the top of our lungs strolling up and down the street. That was great until we scratched all the records.

Much later in our lives, Reuben Saunders became an entertainer in California. He even wrote several songs. Eventually he moved back to Colorado. He had messed up out in California. He had nothing left. He told me he wasted all his money on drugs and alcohol. It was a shame.

We tried to hop the train one time, but it was more fun to put caps on the track. We used to take little dynamite caps and put 'em on the tracks. Bam, bam, bam! We could buy those at the grocery store, too. Sometimes we had to give our money to the other kids to buy us stuff. Ol' Man Benton at the grocery still ran us off. He thought we were going to blow up his store with our water tank rocket.

You ask how we had money. Times were tough. All kids had jobs. I watered, mowed, and kept Dr. Woodard's grass. I shined his shoes for a nickel. Everyone turned in their pennies and nickels to the family fund. Occasionally, Mama gave me a few cents to spend.

Now, there used to be a street car that ran up and down Spruce and Pine. Those older boys used to grease the street car rails when the car was stopped. The perfect location was Costillo Hill. I would like to be clear—I did not participate in these antics, but it sure was fun to watch.

My favorite trick to watch? Those older boys would distract the driver so he stopped the street car. One of the older boys pulled the contact off the overhead wire and swung it away. The driver jumped out of the street car, climbed on the roof, and reattached the contact. One of the boys hopped into the street car, opened the throttle all the way, and scooted off the street car. The moment the driver reconnected the wire, the street car took off. Full speed. Left the driver dangling from the trolley roof.

Street car on the way to the Antler's Hotel in downtown Colorado Springs

Another favorite trick was to force a raw potato into someone's car exhaust pipe. When the engine started, the exhaust pressure built up. In a few seconds, that potato plug blew right out of the tailpipe. ***Bang!***

There was excitement outside of school, but I was getting excited because I was almost ready for Miss Karrison's sixth grade class. I couldn't wait. Experiments. Well, two big things happened in the spring of my fifth grade year. The first one was that they announced the closing of Bristol School for all classes to rebuild the old school.

I was devastated.

I would never have Miss Karrison for sixth grade. All Bristol classes would be enrolled at Washington Elementary.

The second big event was the Flood of 1935. For the town, it was terrible, but Buster and I thought it was great. Let me tell you the story.

Flood of 1935

Buster and I walked down to the railroad bridge. We were just messing around. That flood water came rushing up. We heard a crack. Thankfully, we jumped off the bridge. In seconds, the currents swept the old bridge right down the river. Had we waited one more minute, we would have floated down the river to Pueblo. You would think we would have been scared. We weren't smart enough to recognize the danger. We thought it was tremendous. We watched the bridge crumble and float downstream.

That's how we kicked off our summer.

CHAPTER 10

Greasy Bike and Silent Visitors

Summer went by with our usual antics: carbide experiments and panning for gold. We never did strike it rich, but it sure was fun. By this time, Bobby and I were experts at making dams in the street drainage ditches after it rained. Every street in town was made of dirt, so we had ditches everywhere. We were also whizzes at getting into trouble.

Now Mama, she had arthritis in her hands and ankles. She wasn't going to walk or ride a bike. Through snow, ice, and whatnot, she drove that old Nash car. She'd drive out to the Broadmoor for work. She'd drive to the neighbors'. She'd drive everywhere. There was no such thing as automatic transmission, either. She steered that Nash all over town. Ol' Man Loper couldn't do it, even after our episode at good old Cousin Neck's.

Ol' Man Loper could ride his bike for hours. He could sharp shoot almost anything. He told great stories. Everyone in town loved him. The only thing he couldn't do? **_Drive._** Of course, I didn't mind being the chauffer.

I knew how to drive, and Ol' Man Loper got the ok from the local police. If he was with me, I could drive him around town. No one back then took driver's training. I never took driver's training. Not officially, anyway. I learned from the Warden boys.

In August, I turned 12.

I thought I knew everything. Well, except reading and math. Little did I know I had other troubles a brewin'.

Bristol School was closed for repair. That meant no Miss Karrison's class for me. I was devastated. I had waited since second grade. No telephone-making, no speaker-making, no chemistry, and no *Popular Science* and *Popular Mechanics* magazines. I could hardly believe this was happening.

Frank's new bike (bottom left)

The only good thing about Bristol School closing was that I got a bicycle. I had walked to Bristol, but Washington Elementary was too far. I needed a bicycle.

It was the summer of 1935, and they had just come out with balloon tires. My bike had balloon tires. It was fantastic!

I decided to take the fenders off. I rode around in the rain. That mud went all the way up my back. I put those fenders right back on the bike. It made Ol' Man Loper fall out laughin'.

Mama always made me wash dishes and make lye soap. Making that lye soap was a pain. Mama and Aunt LaLa saved grease over a period of time to mix with the lye. They had this football-shaped tub. It was made of porcelain. I stirred and stirred to combine the grease and the lye. It took forever. When the grease turned white and solidified, it was done. We cut it up into soap bars for washing dishes, taking a bath, and laundry. That old lye soap would clean you up in a heartbeat. You didn't have much skin left, but you were clean.

Being the innovator that I am, I thought, "I'm going to put that bicycle to work."

I put my bicycle on its stand. I set the back wheel in the tub. I hopped on and started peddling. It worked splendidly. No more stirring by hand. I just peddled. That was cookies and ice cream until I had to clean all that grease off my bike. Never occurred to me the melted grease would stick to everything. Let me tell you, getting grease off your bike is not an easy task. I never did that again. Another tremendous idea gone wrong.

I also rode my bike for a job. I delivered shoes for Voorhees Shoe Store. I earned a few cents for each delivery.

By this time, the Wardens had moved away. This meant I couldn't watch Bill Warden fix machines anymore. Alexander Aircraft had already gone out of business due to the Depression. Thankfully, I had Bobby Saunders. My cousins Brother and Buster still lived up the street, but they were more interested in sports.

I was still fascinated with flight. Down the street lived an old coal miner everyone called Black Diamond. I checked in the library archives. I think his last name was Anderson. Ol' Black Diamond had a son named Eugene. I really didn't know Eugene. He was a little older. What I did know was that he built an airplane. Yes, a real true airplane.

Every Sunday when I was supposed to walk up to Reverend Morgan's church for Sunday School, I took a little detour. I turned down the alley to Black Diamond's house. He lived on the 700 block of Spruce Street. There it was. It was beautiful. A real airplane!

For years, I have been trying to find out more about Eugene's airplane. I just remember the day they pulled that thing out of the garage. They placed it onto an old Model A truck bed and drove it up to the old Alexander airstrip. Oh, do I wish I could have seen that craft fly. I was always told it took to the sky just fine.

Of course, I got in trouble for being late to Sunday School, but oh, it was worth it!

Washington Elementary was not for me. We did not do experiments like I had planned.

So I did my own experiments.

There was an old lady up the street who was always dippin' snuff. She had all these snuff cans. I asked her if I could use them for experiments, and she said yes. I mixed carbide and other items to see what would happen. I didn't know the tin itself would react to the carbide. Figured that out fast.

One day I had one of those tins in our front family room. The neighbor John Nichols was over to play with me. Everyone called him Jackie. Anyway, I put a bunch of carbide in the can along with a little something from my chemistry set. Let me tell you, that can took off like a shot! Zoom, across the room. It smashed into the wall behind the curtain. Next thing you know? ***Poof!*** The curtain went up in flames. Fifty years later, Jackie still falls out laughin' about my snuff can experiment.

Speaking of experiments, here's another thing we figured out fast. Airplane wings need struts. Bobby and I were not satisfied with our flight off of the chicken coop. Our carbide rocket never blasted off, so we decided to create our own airplane. After all, Black Diamond's son was doing it. We got some orange crates, took the center section out, and made a seat. We went up the hill by Bristol School. We went zipping down the street. That was fun, but we never took to the air. It was no different than riding on our chugs. That certainly wasn't good enough.

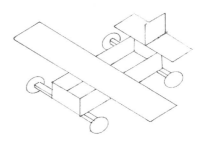

Frank's drawing of Frank and Bobby's orange crate airplane

We decided if we put on wings and a tail section, we should be able to fly. We took bamboo poles and made wings. We covered the wings with flour paste and newspaper, or we covered them with burlap bags. We got more orange crates. We added a tail section. We pulled it with our bicycles. No flight. We pushed it. No flight. We never achieved lift off.

We took this contraption up the clay banks at Uintah Gardens. We figured if we got it going fast enough off the hill, we would fly. Now you need to remember, Pine Street was at the foot of Pikes Peak. Our hills were a little more like cliffs.

Of course, I got in. I was always the test pilot. Down the hill it went. I got great speed. I readied for takeoff when . . . the wings tore right off. I rolled and tumbled. I think the lady who lived up there thought I was dead. Just like any good test pilot, I jumped up and wiped off the dirt. I immediately knew what we needed to do. We needed to go back down the hill and add supports to our wings. Today I know they are called "struts."

Unfortunately, the lady saw us. I think we scared her to death. She witnessed that first crash, and that was it. Somehow that lady got word down to Pine Street. She told Mama and Mrs. Saunders that we were up on the clay banks trying to fly our machine. Mama and Mrs. Saunders were not havin' it. When we came back down to rebuild our plane, they tore that thing right apart. No more flying orange crates for us.

You are probably thinking, "Too bad for Frank and Bobby." Well, we learned a very valuable lesson. Wings need struts.

We had to give up on that endeavor, but I'm thankful to say some of my fellow aviators did not give up on their endeavors. I mentioned General Davis earlier. I am thankful he did not quit. Benjamin O. Davis Jr. graduated from West Point just as I completed the sixth grade. I thought I had it tough in school. Davis had to persevere like no other. No one at West Point would even talk to him. You know what? That did not stop him. He became a four-star general. The best part is he became a pilot.

Frank's signed picture. Benjamin O. Davis is front and center

By this same year, 1936, Amelia Earhart soloed the Atlantic and was preparing for her attempt to circumnavigate the globe. Fortunately for me, aviation was in full swing. You should see some of the airplanes from that time. Some of them were a little wild.

You may laugh at Bobby and me for our airplane inventions, but we were not too far off. The 1909 triplane had wings covered in brown wrapping paper, so our flour paste and newspaper were right on track.

I had plenty of chores to keep me on the ground. Aunt LaLa and Mama sent me around town with a handful of envelopes every month. I walked all around town to pay the bills. It was probably a four-mile trip. One envelope went to the utility company, one went to Benton's Grocery, and so on.

One day, I was out paying the bills. These three older men stopped me and said, "You Charlie's boy?"

I said, "No."

They followed me. Again, they said, "You Charlie's boy?"

I thought for a minute. I wasn't sure what they meant. Then it dawned on me. They were talking about my Grandpa Charlie Banks.

"Oh, you mean Pops, my grandpa? His name is Charlie Banks."

All three nodded. Now I haven't mentioned Charlie Banks yet. I called him Pops for grandpa, and believe it or not, he really was my grandfather. Remember my birth mom's name was Eva Banks?

Let me tell you about Charlie Banks. He, too, was a character. He was a proud Delaware Indian. He'd say, "Delaware Indian from the Algonquin Nation." Now this is important for you to know because he played a little trick before I was born.

His father was White, and his mother was Delaware Indian. They were not married. His mother passed away when he was

Frank's grandpa, "Pops"

little. The tribe wouldn't keep him. His father's family wouldn't take him, either. His dad gave him to an older Black woman on the plantation. I think her last name was Williams.

For years, Pops thought that she was his mom. Somehow there was a big mix-up with his records and with his last name. He came to find out his last name was actually Banks.

Back East, Charlie was going to be rounded up and sent to a reservation because they figured out he was part Delaware Indian.

This practice started back in 1838. It was called the Trail of Tears.

Now Pops was having none of that. Soon as he heard word of that nonsense, he passed himself off as Black. He used the name Williams for the woman who raised him. He signed up to be a Buffalo Soldier. Do you know who the Buffalo Soldiers were? I'll tell you a little about them, but you should look them up.

After the Civil War, the military established cavalry and infantry units of Black soldiers. Pops even went to the Philippine Islands. He caught malaria from a mosquito bite, but by the time I was born, he was just fine. Now there are several stories as to how the name Buffalo Soldier came about. When you look the Buffalo

Soldier history up, you will find that the stories are different, but the title carries great respect.

Buffalo Soldiers

Back to the three gentlemen. I finished paying the bills around town and walked these three men to Pops' house.

I walked in and said to my grandma, "These men are here to see Pops."

My grandma called Pops down from upstairs. He sat in the chair in the front room. The three men sat on the couch directly across from Pops. They all sat there and stared at each other. Not a word was spoken. Thirty minutes later, the three men stood up, nodded, and walked out of the house.

I thought, "What on earth was that all about?"

I asked Pops. He said, "Those are my blood brothers. They came to visit." They, too, were Native Americans. These men were Navajo. As I recall, they went to Manitou Springs to visit sacred grounds.

That was that. I never saw them again.

That was alright—I continued to get in enough trouble with the relatives I knew. With Ol' Man Loper, Mama, and Aunt LaLa, there were no excuses allowed. We were expected to make something of ourselves no matter what. On a patriotic holiday on Sunday, I had to recite Lincoln's *Gettysburg Address* in front of everyone at church. Other times, Mama had me recite parts of *Evangeline* to house guests. Do you know how long that poem is? You should check it out. My point? There was no getting out of getting an education.

As you can expect, I still struggled with my dyslexia at school. I was realizing, however, I had a talent for mechanics and machinery. I encourage you to think about the things you are good at. Work diligently at what is hard, so you start to get it. Work even harder at something you love!

I love to fly. I love to talk about flight. It is a tremendous part of my life. But when I think about it, I still believe my greatest accomplishment was getting through school. If I had never figured out the reading and math thing, I never would have gotten to fly with the Civil Air Patrol or at Tuskegee.

I survived the sixth grade at Washington Elementary. Riding my bike to school was the real highlight of the year. As usual, I had a few notes sent home for various mischievous events. That led to a few spankings and a lot of singing "Amazing Grace" with Mama.

Aunt JuJu still ratted me out as often as she could. Aunt LaLa still went after the chickens, and Mama tried her best to make me respectable.

Life on Pine Street was good.

CHAPTER 11

Sulfur and a Sunkin' Nash

We weren't done with the flying. Oh, no. That bicycle I had? Well, I started riding it down to the Rocky Mountain airfield. There were several airstrips in Colorado Springs. When Alexander Aircraft went out of business, I started going to the airstrip southeast of town.

I swept and cleaned the airplanes. When I did that, the pilots would take me flying. I had to earn nine dollars for a real one-hour flight with a lesson. The nine dollars included aircraft use, fuel, and instruction. In 1936, that was a lot of money. Today that is equivalent to one hundred and fifty-five dollars per hour. It was almost impossible for me to have that much money at one time. Just to put it into perspective, my nine dollars for flying could pay the whole month utility bill. Thankfully, I could save four dollars and fifty cents and do some extra cleaning and get a half-hour flight. It was fabulous.

Bobby and I bought models of airplanes. We never left them in their original form. Our innovative minds always thought of ways to improve on the design. We whittled, cut, glued—whatever it took to get the best possible result.

Speaking of the best possible result, this was the year my Uncle Herman and I did some experimenting. I think Herman was really a cousin, but I called him Uncle Herman. I was finally old enough for Mama and Aunt LaLa to allow me to ride the street car. That was funny to me. I had been driving since I was six.

Anyway, I hopped on the street car at Spruce Street and Monument. I rode it all the way to Manitou Springs. That's where Herman lived. Herman had a chemistry set just like I did. He also had a whole swarm of bees living in his chimney. Every time Herman's mom built a fire in the fireplace, honey oozed down and dripped in the flames.

Herman and I decided to take care of this little problem. It was a great engineering opportunity. We headed up to his room to figure out the best chemical solution from his chemistry set. We mixed. We stirred. We tested. We created the smokiest option possible. Our plan? Fog those bees right out of the fireplace flue.

As you might guess, we decided the chemistry set needed a little extra. We didn't have any carbide. On this particular day, we had sulfur. We made our own concoction. It smoked alright. It fogged out the whole house. It smelled like a thousand rotten eggs. There were all kinds of commotion when we did our test run. Smoke filled the entire house. Herman's mom ran to his room, just hollering and flailing she came up so fast. She may not have even touched the stairs. Of course, we got chastised. We never even got to try our brilliant chemical creation on the bees.

In terms of life at school, I'm proud to say that I made it through elementary school. That was a small miracle.

No, that was a huge miracle.

I had six years of school to go. I wasn't sure I would make it, but I knew Mama wouldn't let me quit.

To tell you the truth, I had so much to learn from my own struggles and experiments that I still wasn't aware of the great conflicts building in the world. Little did I know, we were three years away from Germany invading Poland. If you didn't know, that is what started World War II. I **_did_** know I was going to fly. I wanted to be a pilot.

However, I could barely read on my own. I was still using my fingers to run along the words. I was getting a little better. You couldn't ask me to read a novel, but I read those _Popular Science_ magazines all the time. They had pictures.

I was ready to head off to North Junior High. I had just celebrated my thirteenth birthday. Then something wonderful happened. Actually, two wonderful things happened.

The first thing was something that the whole world knew about. The Olympic runner and athlete Jesse Owens stunned the world. He won four gold medals for the United States in three days. All the kids in the neighborhood, well, we thought we were Jesse Owens! We raced and raced.

The second great thing was that I went to North

Jesse Owens, 1936 Olympics

Junior High School four weeks after my birthday. You know what happened? I signed up for an elective. That means a class of your choice. I signed up for mechanical drawing. It changed my life.

I was good at mechanical drawing. Suddenly, I had a reason to try hard in school. I kept practicing my reading using my fingers to keep the words from jumping all over the place. I read instruction manuals instead of novels. For the first time in my life, I started to read on my very own. There still are many times I have to read and reread to understand. That is exactly what I did back then. I did it because I was determined to do it on my own.

I wasn't bored at school, so I didn't do things like put pepper in the teacher's chocolate-covered cherries like I did in second grade. Now don't get me wrong, I still suffered, but the mechanical drawing class made it worth it.

Oh man, did I suffer in math. At this point, I was still counting on my fingers. Let me tell you something: by the time you reach seventh grade, you run out of fingers. The numbers get too big. I had to do something. I had a very good memory, so I started memorizing the math facts I should have learned in elementary. Now, they didn't always make sense, but I memorized. I suggest you do it, too. It will make your life much easier when you are an adult.

I knew I wasn't any good at a problem with multiple numbers. Because of the dyslexia I didn't know I had, those numbers jumped around just like the letters. I figured out I was good at patterns. Once I memorized my math facts, I picked out patterns. The easiest patterns for me to find were doubles and combinations that added up to 5's and 10's.

Here. Let me show you. If I have a simple problem like $4+5$, it is not too bad. I know that $5+5=10$. Doubles are the easiest for me. So, in my head, I say, "If $5+5$ is 10, then $4+5$ is one less than 10, which equals 9." I don't always recognize that $4+5=9$ without doing the $5+5=10$ first.

Now, when a problem gets harder, I follow the same system. I matched up all numbers that equal 10 first. I italicized the numbers I would match up together. Like this.

4+5+*1*   In my head or on paper, I move the 1 over by the 4.

4+*1*(5)+5=10   Now I know that 4+1 is 5 and 5+5=10.

Here's another example problem:

6+3+7+4+5+5=   In my head, I add all combinations of 10.

6+4 3+7 5+5   Now I can see I have 3 sets of 10, which equals 30.

Today, I even do this with license plates to practice my math. I form patterns all the time. Now this is another example. Since this was the year, I am proud to say, I memorized multiplication and division math facts. I can see doubles patterns, too.

Pretend this is a license plate:

13467   My brain tells me I have two options. I can add to 10 like this:

3+7 6+4 (1)   That works, but the 1 is extra. You must remember to add it.

Remember I told you I was good at doubles after I learned my math facts? Well, now I can see a different pattern. Can you see it? Instead of adding up to 10, I can see 7 as a pattern. Let me show you.

Now I can see I have 3 sets of 7. Because I memorized my math facts, I know 7+7+7=21 or 7x3=21.

I must do this when I have a harder problem, too. Let me show you.

$$
\begin{array}{r}
5552 \\
2379 \\
5412 \\
+8525 \\
\hline
\end{array}
$$

I start with the right-hand column. I see 9 and 3 numbers that add up to 9. Two 9's=18. Write 8, carry the 1.

Second column, I see 5 and 3 numbers that add up to 10. So, 5+10=15. Add the carried 1, and write a 6. Carry the next 1.

In the third column, two 5's make 10. 4+1 makes a 5. So, 10+5 is 15, add 3. That is 18. Write the 8, carry the next 1.

In the last column, I see two 5's, which equal 10. Also, 2+8=10. Two 10's=20, and add the 1. Write 21 below the column.

21,868.

Now, division is always the hardest for me, even today. But I don't let that stop me.

Enough about math.

Buster and Brother started liking the girls in the neighborhood, and Bobby and I still wanted to experiment with machinery. We found ways to combine our interests.

We used to have neighborhood parties. There were two kids who never got invited. That was Brother Moore and me. Brother was always into something. Of course, I was too. Most times we were in it together. We were the ones who put leaves in between the screen door and main door of the neighborhood houses on Halloween. Stuff like that. Brother and I did the pranks around the neighborhood. Bobby Saunders and I experimented. We were the innovators.

The neighborhood kids knew we wouldn't go along with their plans, so they didn't invite us. That was just fine. We had better things to do. What the other kids didn't know was we had an informant. Buster Moss.

At these parties, they played this game called "Spin the Bottle." You were supposed to kiss a girl when the bottle pointed her way. We didn't want to do that.

Naturally, we brought some carbide to put in the bottle. Carbide always made a good distraction.

When no one was looking, in to the bottle went the carbide. It was great! We spit in there to get the gases going. Someone in the neighborhood would spin the bottle. The spinning shook up the carbide, and then we would light a match. That bottle would send out a huge amount of smelly gas and shoot across the room. End of that party.

The other kids didn't think much of that.

Now my cousin Buster Moss, he never got in trouble. Oh, don't let him fool you. He did naughty stuff; he just got away with it. Since we didn't tell on him, he always made sure we knew about the parties. I think Buster used us for entertainment. Just Brother Moore and I walking in could end the party, and Buster thought that was hilarious.

It was fine with us. Those parties were so boring. Kind of like school during my elementary years. Who wants to spin a bottle just to kiss a girl?

Now some kids think parties are just great. I was more interested in the balsa wood gliders. We got them from the gas station. They were much better than the Little Orphan Annie decoder rings. The gliders even had a diagram of a cockpit. I thought, "Now we're talking."

Bobby Saunders and I were never quite satisfied with drawings or models. We loved them, but we always thought we could do better. Make improvements, you know. I was thirteen. Still thought I knew everything.

Around this time, the Saunders boys and I built a raft. We drew up our plan and started building. We used logs, rope, whatever we could get our hands on. We completed our masterpiece, loaded it on our wagon, and hauled it to the railroad tracks. Gettin' that thing over the tracks was a feat of its own. Well, we made it. Off to Monument Park Lake. We had to test our raft.

We climbed aboard and headed out into the water. We reached the center of the lake. It was our first transportation success. Or so we thought. That old raft fell apart. Bobby, Ted, Reuben, and I were soaked. Luckily, we each grabbed a log and kicked back to the shore.

The old park supervisor was not sympathetic at all.

Off to our next project.

The old telephones were placed on the wall. First, to operate the phone, you had to crank a magnet to generate the electrical energy to cause the signal to transfer down the phone line. These phones were replaced by a newer type that did not need the magnets. What to do with the discarded phones? Simple. Take the wire and phone and head to the lake. Drop that wire in the water and turn the crank. It stuns the fish. They come up to the surface, eyes as wide as they could go. However, do not put your hand in the water to pick them up. You, too, will get shocked. We learned this the hard way because we headed straight to the park and dipped the wires in the lake.

Once again, the park manager was not impressed.

For the first time in my life, school started to make sense. I really had to work, but I finally had something I enjoyed. Along with the mechanical drawing, I took weather. I took wood working and ancient history. The choice of history might seem strange, but I always had a fascination with Ancient Egypt. I think it was from the museum in San Francisco.

Now, ancient history intrigued me. Current events not as much. Do you remember me telling you all kinds of events happen around you, and you don't even realize? Well, that was happening in my life just as it is in yours.

This was also the year Cornelius Coffey, another great aviator, developed a heated carburetor. What does that mean? Airplanes could now fly in all weather conditions. That means, if you have ever been in an airplane at night or in the winter, Cornelius's invention changed your life.

Cornelius Coffey, great inventor and aviator

The other thing I would like you to know about Cornelius Coffey is that he was the first Black man to hold both a pilot's license and a mechanic's license. This is important to me because I spent twenty-three years as an airplane mechanic.

1936 was also the year I decided to take the old Nash for a leisurely drive.

Just to clarify, Ol' Man Loper got the ok for me to drive him around town. He did not get the ok for me to go out driving with my friends. An adult in our family had to be in the car with me.

That didn't stop me.

Mr. and Mrs. Roberts, friends of the family, won a car. Yes, they won a car. They came by and took Mama and Aunt LaLa for a ride. As I remember, Dad (Ol' Man Loper) was working out of town. He would go on out-of-town jobs. I remember because he always reminded me I was the "Man of the House." Naturally, I took my position very seriously.

I do not remember why I was not invited to go with the Roberts, Mama, and LaLa. I guess it was a break for the adults. At this point, the Wardens had moved away. Remember, Brother Bill and Uncle Bill Warden were the ones who originally taught me to drive. I figured I was the "Man of the House," so why not go for a ride in the old Nash? No one was around, so I figured that left me in charge.

The 1929 Nash was sitting in the garage. I decided to drive it out of the garage and go cruising. I let some of the neighbor kids go with me on the epic ride. Now this was late summer or early fall. What you must know about Colorado is that rain or snow can come up in a second. It can rain like crazy. Just as quick, it can disappear.

We all hopped in the car. I think there were about six of us. We drove up Pine to Willamette and back down Walnut. We were having a grand time. It started to rain. Oh man, did it rain! The neighbor kids were hangin' out of the window and everything. We all thought it was great. Then, we turned the corner, and I spotted Mama and LaLa coming back down the street in the Roberts' car. I should have been terrified. I wasn't smart enough for that.

I just thought, "Oh boy, I have to get home before they do."

Now you must picture the problem I faced. The garage entrance was in the alley. The alley laid between our back fence and the railroad bed. The railroad bed was about five feet above the alley. It was all dirt. After the torrential rain we just had, that dirt was not dirt. It was mud. The mud was not the only problem. To get the old Nash back in the garage, you had to swing around the telephone pole that stood at the end of the drive. I couldn't go in from the other angle. Mama and LaLa were coming in from that way.

Normally, it took several tries to get in and out of our garage. I did not have that kind of time. To eliminate all the turning and backing in and out, I thought out a solution. I figured if I drove up on the railroad bed, I could miss the pole and swing wide enough to come down straight into the garage.

I hit the gas. I flew up the railroad bed and got halfway into my turn on the side of the five-foot berm. I buried that old Nash fifteen inches down in the mud. I could not get it to move. The more the wheels spun, the deeper in the mud the car went. I was stuck!

Since it was Sunday afternoon, the whole neighborhood was home. Everyone came out to see what the noise was all about.

Now Mama and Aunt LaLa arrived just in time to see the Nash stuck to its axles. Thankfully, all the other kids had hopped out and ran like crazy. They knew all involved would be in "deep yogurt," as we used to say.

Mama and Aunt LaLa showed up to see what was going on behind their house.

LaLa's first comment was, "Boy, that train is gonna come by here and suck that car right up under it."

Being a brilliant thirteen-year-old, I replied, "It sure would have to do a lot of suckin' to do that."

To get the old Nash off the railroad bed, we once again had to go down to Farmer Reed's. He harnessed up those trusty work horses and pulled the Nash off the railbed and into the alley.

I spent hours getting the mud off that old car. Plus, Aunt LaLa didn't forget the "suckin'" comment.

Weeks later when Ol' Man Loper came home, he heard all the details of my drive. Mama and Aunt LaLa were still hoppin' mad. They told him the tale, thinking he would be mad, too.

He cracked up laughing.

Now he was the one in trouble.

CHAPTER 12

Tragedy and the Goat

The escapades of summer were coming to a close. I guess after driving around the 1929 Nash and getting it stuck, it was safer for me to be in school. Now I was not as mischievous during school because I started to like my classes. Remember me talking about ancient history in the last chapter? I dreamed of having one of those beetles found in Ancient Egypt. I also dreamed of flying.

I decided if I didn't have the money to fly in a plane all the time, I might as well fly on my bike. North Junior had a large area that was part of the soccer field. At the north end was an impression. It was a deep dip that served as a drain ditch. I peddled my bike as fast as I could. I hit the edge and flew over the ditch. The goal? Hit the ditch and see how far I could fly. That was all great until the day my classmates tried this little stunt. One of the boys did not make it to the other side. He got hurt. Probably broke something. You know what happened next. That was the end of bike jumping for Franklin. I wasn't even the one who crashed. Mama and Aunt

LaLa somehow figured I gave the neighborhood kids the idea. I never did such a thing. They copied me. I just thought it would be fun.

I mentioned earlier that there were places in town that were segregated. The one I do recall was the local pool. We could go in the wading pool, but we couldn't go in the big pool. At the time, I just thought it was a stupid rule. I thought it was because we were kids, not because of our skin color.

We made our fun anyway. We played in the wading pool as if it were an Olympic arena. I thought I was a lifeguard. I truly believed I could swim. One day we went up to Denver. We were visiting our Denver cousins. We headed to the Black YMCA. The Y had a ten-foot pool. I jumped right in the far end. I figured I could handle the deep. That was a big mistake. I needed to touch the bottom to be in a pool.

My cousin Jimmy hollered, "I thought you could swim."

I hollered and sputtered, "I _can_ in the wading pool."

He jumped in and grabbed me. It was too deep for me to kick off the bottom and get going. I'm just glad he didn't drop me back in and let me sink.

I really thought I could swim. I was so embarrassed.

Later, I learned how to swim and do some fancy diving off the diving board.

Back in Colorado Springs, eighth grade was off to a good start. I took metal shop, wood working, and mechanical drawing to name a few. English was still tough, but I excelled in mechanical drawing. This was the year I began to question a few things. I wondered about my real dad.

Mama always told me James Macon, her first husband, was my father. I didn't question Mama until I saw her first husband's name, James Macon, under "Deaths" in Mama's old family Bible, the one used to prove my birth. They used to tell me he was my daddy. Then I realized he died three years before I was born. That really confused me.

I thought, "That's impossible."

The other thing I realized was that many elementary classmates stopped going to school. In 1937, it was a luxury to go to school past the sixth or seventh grade. In my town, if you were poor, you had to drop out. Why? You had to go to work and help support the family. Now don't get things wrong. Some people today assume that only meant the Black kids or something. Well, let me tell you, that is not true. There were many poor White kids who dropped out to work for the family. Poor kids period. It didn't matter what color you were. This probably would surprise many people today.

Now we did not have extra money, but we were middle class. So were all my cousins who lived in the neighborhood. We always had food, shelter, and clothing. The adults in my life had jobs. I know of men who joined the Civil Conservation Corps Camps and later went directly into the service when World War II began. I was not in that situation. Ol' Man Loper was a self-made man. He lost most of what he earned in the 1929 crash, but by the time I was in eighth grade, he owned a number of properties. I even had two pairs of shoes. One pair for playing and going to school. The second pair for going to church.

By this time, I knew I had to make something of myself. It didn't matter that I had trouble with reading and math. It didn't matter that I still wasn't sure about my real mother and father. It didn't matter that the world had great tensions. Mama set high standards. Ol' Man Loper followed suit. That meant I would make something of myself. Of course, Mama wanted me to play piano and become a preacher. She never understood the flying.

This reminds me of a story. I have to tell you about a boy in my class. His name was Nat.

Nat was one of those kids who had the fancy clothes and car when we got in high school. He teased me for working at the garage and for trying to do well in school. Nat's mother worked hard. She gave him everything. He drove around with the girls. He thought he was great, but he was **_lazy_**. He did nothing except mock me and the other kids who worked. His mother never made him do a thing. He was what you would call "flashy."

Later in life, he married my cousin Mamiebell. I remember Mamiebell and her brother. They were terrific athletes. Mamiebell took care of Nat. He went from his momma taking care of him to Mamiebell taking care of him. That meant he still didn't have to do much of anything. He didn't.

He used to tease me because I didn't dress so well. Blue jeans and a sweatshirt.

Frank on the right in his jeans and sweatshirt, having fun with the neighbors

I always had grease under my fingers from working at the garage. He even called me "Whitey." For some reason, he thought working hard at school meant I was trying to be White or something like that. I worked hard because I watched Mama, Aunt LaLa, and Ol' Man Loper work their tails off, and I watched them succeed. They were tremendous people. I wanted to make them proud. That's exactly what I did.

I just didn't like that attitude. The one like Nat's. I still don't like that attitude. He never did anything. He wasted his talents.

Years later, I ran into him. I didn't even know who he was. Mamiebell had kicked him out. She got sick and tired of him doing nothing. She worked hard. He wasted their money. He wore messy old clothes. No more fancy stuff. The money was long gone. He just played and squandered all his opportunities.

Thirty years later, Nat started telling me, "I wish I had gone to school" and on and on.

Now here he was. His mother would do anything for him to go to college or technical training. He had every opportunity I had. Like Ol' Man Loper used to say, "You either _**do**_ or you _**don't do**_. There is no _**try**_."

Well, Nat _**didn't do**_ anything productive. What he did do was drive around with the girls and mock those of us who were trying to get an education. By the time I saw him, we were adults. I was a pilot and a mechanic and worked for an aviation research company.

Old Nat wasn't teasing me anymore. I had the last laugh. I tell you this because you can't let someone stop you from using your full potential. If they tease you, prove them wrong. If you are the one doing the teasing, get with the program and make something of yourself!

Life started to look up. At least when it came to school. Now, don't let me fool you. I was the first one out of the door when that old bell rang. I had other things to do. But I was at least making some progress with my reading and math.

I could finally read on my own. Now, I might have had to read something three times, but I could do it. Eighth grade was going very well until late fall.

Something was coming that was even worse than my dyslexia or not having Miss Karrison for sixth grade.

Ol' Man Loper was a great storyteller. He always had a job, so he was well known around town. The last job he held was at the Colorado Springs Fine Arts Center. Like I mentioned in an earlier chapter, he always looked good. He learned from the businessmen and became successful. He owned a number of properties. Now, you already know he was a terrible driver. He never did learn to drive. Instead, he rode his bicycle. Ol' Man Loper peddled and his dog, Blanyo, trotted behind him.

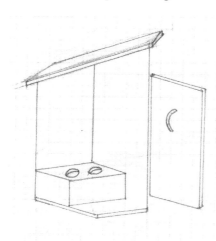

Frank's drawing of the outhouse built by Ol' Man Loper for the rental houses

He owned several houses. He had two houses next to each other. I think he built them from scratch. One was large, and one was small. In between the two houses was the outside toilet. Oh man, did those outhouse holes stink in the hot summer sun.

The two families would use this outhouse. Later he built the bathroom onto the house. I tell this because Ol' Man Loper spent his last night at these properties.

That October, the people moved out of Ol' Man Loper's rental house. He loved to paint, so he decided to paint the house again. Back then, they used calcimine (or whitewash). It was basically water and lime, I think. He stayed over there Friday night to paint. He slept there. I remember that night because Mama made him dinner and brought it over to the house for him. He and the dog and his bicycle stayed overnight.

The next morning, he headed to work. On his way, he stopped at Murray Drug on Tejon and Dale Street. He went to cash his check and dropped dead in the drug store. They called Mama. She called for the funeral home, and she sent me to get the bicycle. That old police dog Blanyo wouldn't let me on that bike.

So I tricked him. Finally, I did. I hopped on the bicycle, and Blanyo followed me home. I was shocked, but you do what you have to do. Old Man Loper was a wonderful man.

Now a couple weeks later, that old dog disappeared. The story goes, they found old Blanyo on Ol' Man Loper's grave. How he found that grave, I will never know.

Sometimes people ask me, "How old was Frank Loper when he died?" Well, that we will never know, either. I told you earlier he was born on Jefferson Davis's plantation. During the Civil War, all the papers burned. Ol' Man Loper was quoted in the paper one time. The newspaper made it sound like Ol' Man Loper couldn't speak properly. This is what it said:

"'Ah don' know how old Ah is,' 'Uncle Frank' used to recall, 'but Ah was quite a boy when Grant took Richmond and that was Fourth of July in 1863. His soldiers burnt all Mistah Jefferson Davis' papers, so Ah don' know my age.'"

He would say he remembered his mother told him he was born on a Sunday in May. Ol' Man Loper did not know which one, so we celebrated on every Sunday of that month. It was fantastic.

Now I must tell you about this newspaper quote. It is true that Ol' Man Loper did not know his birthday, but he did not speak in the pidgin English used in the newspaper. Mama would not be acquainted with such improper grammar. *The Gazette* wanted to make it look like Ol' Man Loper was not educated. He was. The Davis family made sure he could read, write, and speak proper English.

The Gazette ran this very nice article about Ol' Man Loper when he passed. The only problem was that they made it look like he talked in pidgin English. Now, he was fluent in English, Creole, and Cajun, but Frank Loper did not speak in pidgin English. Let me tell you what! Maude Elizabeth Macon-Loper

Frank's favorite picture of Ol' Man Loper

was **_not_** having any of that. She marched straight down to the newspaper. She let them have it. Well, she did not get the result she wanted. She wanted the paper to change the quote to read in proper English. She was proud of her husband and the educations they both had earned. The paper did not respond.

Do you think that stopped her? **_No!_**

The very next day, Mama, accompanied by Jefferson Hayes-Davis, went straight back to *The Gazette*. Let me tell you, the correction, or retraction, as it is called in the newspaper world, was written. It was in the back, but it was there. Mama and the Davis family made sure of that.

Ol' Man Loper's death was very hard for me. Ol' Man Loper was a father to me. Our family had to cope with this tragedy the best that we could.

Earlier in 1937, when I was finishing up seventh grade, aviation had two tragedies as well. How well do you know your aviation history? I will give you a couple of clues. The first happened in May 1937. The aircraft left from Germany and was supposed to land in New Jersey. Can you guess what it is?

Hindenburg disaster

It was the Hindenburg. Zeppelin airships were becoming popular ways for people to fly. The Hindenburg was a massive airship. Unfortunately, something terrible happened upon the landing.

Ironically, another tragedy in aviation was about to happen. It may be one of the most famous stories because no one knows the answer to the question, "What happened?"

Just days after the Hindenburg exploded, Amelia Earhart set out to fly around the world. She and her navigator, Fred Noonan, took off on May 21, 1937. On July 18, 1937, Amelia Earhart was declared lost at sea. She and Fred had left the city of Lae in the country of New

Guinea on July 2, 1937. They never made it to their next refueling stop on Howland Island. Today, it is still a mystery.

Paul Mantz, Amelia Earhart, Fred Noonan, and Harry Manning in front of Earhart's Lockheed 10E Electra

I certainly don't want you to think things are always bad. Some very good things also happened at this time. Now the world was building up to World War II, but I was still building contraptions. Believe it or not, I was getting more advanced. Bobby and I had a lot of scientific failures, but each one taught us something new. We made so many things that I was becoming good at building and fixing real things, like automobiles. I finished eighth grade, and I got a job at Jack Hanthorn's garage.

At first, I cleaned tools. Back then, you cleaned tools in gasoline. That is not a great idea. I made a spark one day and set the place on fire. Luckily, it was a small fire.

I chased parts for them as well. That means that I had to find the correct parts in the stock pile of parts.

One part of my job was driving the boss home. Old Jack was a big drinker. I drove him home each night. Probably the main reason I never took up drinkin'.

Eventually I got so good at fixing cars Judge McGeery would have those policemen come by the shop. It was not because I was in trouble. He just wanted me to fix his stuff. He knew I was very good at it.

Those officers always said jokingly, "Judge McGeery said you was speeding."

I laughed and said, "What does he need fixed now?"

Usually, it was his old car.

Oh man, the judge was a huge guy. The springs in his car seats busted all the time. He had this old boat he wanted fixed or painted. It didn't make any difference. If he wanted something fixed, he sent the police over to give me "a ticket." My fine was to go to the judge's house and fix his stuff, or he would come down to Hanthorn's Garage for me to work on his old car. I took it as an honor because the judge believed in my skills.

I must tell you two funny stories. It didn't happen until I was finished at Tuskegee College, but it happened at Jack Hanthorn's garage.

Jack's garage was located on Spruce Street. Across the street was Fisher's Conoco Filling Station and a little liquor store. Ol' Fisher was always about "three sheets to the wind," as the old folks would say. That means he was drunk. He always came over there to Jack's, dumping all his trash in the doorway of the garage. Of course, I always cleaned this mess up. Youngest on the payroll got the dirty job. I tired of this, so I figured out a plan.

The war effort was going on. At that time, you could contribute money to war bonds. One of the prizes donated for buying war bonds was a goat.

Ol' Jack won the goat. He had me drive out into the country and fetch that animal.

I drove that Model A pickup out to the country. I got that goat up in there. I brought it to Jack's shop. I was sick and tired of Fisher putting trash in Jack's garage, so I got there early in the morning and tied that goat up to Fisher's gas pump with a long rope. I hoped the goat would keep Ol' Fisher from dumping his trash at Jack's Garage. Well, Ol' Fisher was drunk as usual. He came to work, but he never saw the goat. That goat took out after him. Trash went flying and Ol' Fisher ran like crazy. Jack just fell out laughing. Ol' Fisher never put trash at Jack's again. The best part? Everyone in the neighborhood knew about Fisher and that goat. He got teased about that old goat for the rest of his life.

There was also an old drunk guy who came into Jack's to use the toilet. The bathroom was in the basement. He messed all over everything. I tired of that, too. I was always the one cleaning.

Now, I don't think it was my idea, but it worked like a charm. I took some copper plating down to the toilet. I strung wire around that toilet seat and up the stairs. I connected the wire up to a spark plug tester. If you know anything about a spark plug tester, it checks for an electrical charge. Well, this old man went stumbling down the stairs one day. I waited about three minutes, and I flipped that tester on. **_Zap!_** That old drunk flew up the stairs and he never came back. I never cleaned up his mess again.

Enough about the later years. Back to eighth grade. I finally finished junior high the spring of 1938. I continued to bike to the airfield every chance I got. And like most young boys, I sprinted out of school as fast as I could. Luckily for me, I had a place to go: Jack Hanthorn's auto shop.

CHAPTER 13

Mama Was Right, Mr. Hale Was Wrong

We had only one public high school in the immediate Colorado Springs area in 1938. We were known as the "Terrors."

The high school today is called Palmer High School, after General Palmer. The high school still has students, and they are still the "Terrors." Last fall I was inducted into their Hall of Fame. Can you believe that? I know Mr. Hale, the mechanics teacher, would never have believed it.

Just like in junior high, we were allowed to have several elective subjects. My first year, I, of course, picked auto mechanics, mechanical drawing, and chemistry.

I tried out for football. I was on the team for part of one season. I very quickly found out football was not my thing. I was way too small in weight, so I headed back to the gymnastics team.

Frank standing in the front yard of his home on Pine Street after getting home from school and work at the garage

As I mentioned earlier, it is good to try different things. How else would you find out what you are best suited for? (Just for the record, this does _**not**_ apply to things that are detrimental. That means bad for you or your future.)

The elective subjects I selected were very interesting to me, so I was not bored. Since I wasn't bored, I did not get into much trouble. Well, except for the prank I played on Mr. Hale, my auto mechanics teacher.

Mr. Hale always played pranks on the students. He pulled one on me, so I got him back. I should have known better than to get even, but he deserved it.

I got him back by wiring up his chair to the spark plug tester. He was not amused. He marched me in front of the principal. I thought I was in for it.

I told the principal, "He pulled a prank on me. If he wanted to play that way, he should expect to get it right back."

The principal thought I had a valid point and just told me not to do it again.

I couldn't get out of school fast enough. I ran straight to Jack Hanthorn's Garage when that final bell rang. Let me tell you something funny about my job at Jack's. Mr. Hale, the teacher whose chair I hooked up to the spark plug tester, told me all year long I wouldn't be able to be a mechanic. He tried to discourage me by telling me I could not get a job as an auto mechanic due to my color.

He said, "Franklin, you'll only be able to wash and polish cars."

I just smiled at him.

Yet another person telling me I could not do things. Little did he know, I had plenty of people telling me I ***could*** be a mechanic. Funny thing, while Mr. Hale tried to stop me, the country moved in a very different direction. That spring of 1939, the Army Expansion Act passed. Shortly after, the Civilian Pilot Training Act was approved. The making of Tuskegee, where I would eventually go to flight school, was on its way.

I just thought Mr. Hale didn't know what he was talking about. I never told him that after school and on Saturdays I learned to be an auto mechanic at Jack Hanthorn's. Jack paid me, too! I just told Ol' Mr. Hale I wanted to know how to fix my own car. That way he left me alone.

My prank wasn't even the best part. You see, some of those mechanics at Jack's had had Mr. Hale for a teacher. I told them what he said about not being able to be a mechanic. Oh, they did not like that. Ol' Jack was, as they used to say, "a true Irishman." He sported a temper. He was not going to let any auto mechanics teacher stop me or talk bad to me.

Now for the fun I had with Mr. Hale. Those mechanics at Jack's who'd had Mr. Hale as their teacher informed me of all his test tricks. They made sure I was well prepared for every single quiz and test. Now don't think we were cheating. Everything was hands on for those mechanics tests.

Those men set an engine on a stand for me to practice.

I practiced and practiced.

They all knew that Mr. Hale would use a star engine from an old car. He would make the test so difficult anyone who hadn't practiced like I had wouldn't know what was coming for them. He would remove the spark plug wires and hand them to the student to replace them in the proper order. He would try to trick us, too. He would turn the crankshaft over and remove the distributor. It made you lose the timing marks.

You might think that's not a big deal. Let me tell you, if the wires were not placed in the proper order, the engine wouldn't run. The worst part was you would have to hand crank it in front of all your classmates. If the wires were in the wrong order, the engine would backfire and tear that hand crank right out of your hands. It hurt! It could even break your arm.

One of the mechanics at Jack's was named Pete. He wasn't so fond of Ol' Mr. Hale, so Pete took it upon himself to help me handle my mechanics teacher. Pete told me just how to accomplish the task. He said Mr. Hale may take the distributor out and turn the engine over so all the timing marks would no longer be in line.

Pete pointed out, "Here is how to find the timing marks."

Armed with all this information, I was well prepared for every test and exam.

As Pete said, he pulled that on all of us. Pete was more than happy to help me out and pull something over on Mr. Hale.

Oh, was Mr. Hale upset when I replaced everything perfectly and cranked that engine up. That engine fired up effortlessly. Mr. Hale even tried to get me to tell him how I knew the tricks and how I fixed it correctly.

I just said, "Lucky, I guess."

I never told my secret.

Pete and Riley down at the shop had also "schooled" me on all of Mr. Hale's pranks. I knew what was coming. Now that I'm older, I realize it is just better to not say anything and outsmart 'em.

Years later, I ran into Mr. Hale at the auto parts store. He asked me if I was working on my car. I informed him I was picking up some parts for Hanthorn's shop. I was employed. I had worked there since I was in junior high school as an apprentice mechanic and now as a full-time mechanic.

It was tremendous to see the look on his face!

He didn't believe me, but the auto parts store confirmed my story. They

Frank speaking to freshman history classes at the United States Air Force Academy

laughed about it when I told them the story of Mr. Hale not wanting me to succeed in his class.

High school moved right along. Mama and Aunt LaLa still tried to keep me in line. Now I was doing better. No notes home from school. I still fixed and built things. I was also expected to recite poetry at church and for company. Oh man, did I hate that!

I told you Mama made me read *Evangeline*, as well as memorize *The Gettysburg Address* and other poetry and Bible selections. I thought this was the worst thing a young man of his teenage years could do.

It was awful, but once again, Mama was right. Today, I am ever so thankful. I think that is one of the reasons I can get up and speak to any crowd. It does not make me one bit nervous. Now, I speak all over the place. I will be honest with you, it does scare mc to read in front of a group due to my dyslexia. But a speech? Oh, that's simple.

I really am a private person, but I learned to share my story. We all have an important story if we take advantage of our opportunities. You can even look up my name on the Internet and find some newspaper articles.

Mama never dreamed I would be in front of so many people talking about history. But I sure am. I go to all kinds of elementary schools. I even speak at places like the United States Air Force Academy. I know Mama is proud.

Frank's introduction to thousands of cadets, Mitchell Hall,
United States Air Force Academy–a standing ovation

There is another thing to which I attribute my ability to speak and do it well. I am a relative of Frederick Douglass. That's right. The great grandmother of Mama, Aunt LaLa, and Clara (Eva's mother) was a half-sister to the Great Orator.

The way I figured it, talking is in the blood. If you do not know much about Frederick Douglass, I think you should look him up for yourself. He was born a slave. He escaped slavery and became a great speaker, writer, and trusted advisor to Abraham Lincoln. He contributed and used his talents in many great ways.

Frank "shaking hands" with Frederick Douglass

Here's my favorite quote of his: "What is possible for me is possible for you."

I love this quote because I think the same is true for all of us; if we stop feeling sorry for ourselves and believe in ourselves and find our talents, we accomplish many things.

Back to high school.

All through high school, I worked at Jack Hanthorn's garage. Mama and Aunt LaLa tried to keep track of me. I can't remember if I had any spankings. You probably think I was too old. Think again. Not for Aunt LaLa.

I still rode my bike to the airfield as often as I could. When I saved up four dollars and fifty cents, Dorothy Jones gave me a short flying lesson. If I managed to save up the whole nine dollars, I got the full lesson. After all, I was not giving up on my dream to be a pilot.

It was 1940. I kept designing airplanes. I would use my money from my job at Jack's and buy model airplane kits. I designed and reworked the planes. Of course, I crashed them. That was part of the fun. It helped me learn the concepts of flight.

Once, my friend Dick Erwin and I took those model airplanes to North Junior and flew them across the auditorium. Naturally, we got detention.

My math skills were still atrocious, but with something like mechanical drawing, boom! I drew up anything.

My second year of high school was another turning point in my life. It was for many young men and women in this country. That September, Germany invaded Poland to begin World War II.

At this point, America was not in the war, but that was coming.

I finished my sophomore and began my junior year of high school. I still spent most of my time at Jack's or at the airfield. Now I'm going to cut to the chase. I don't want a chapter that is too long. The point here is that, while I was finishing high school, things at Tuskegee were just getting started.

The summer before my senior year, on July 19, 1941, the first class, 42-C, entered preflight at Tuskegee. By November, the Ninety-ninth Pursuit Squadron moved from Maxwell Field, Alabama to Tuskegee Army Airfield, Alabama.

My senior year began. Believe it or not, I had not even heard of Tuskegee, but they were hard at work. On December 3, 1941, Major Noel F. Parrish transferred command from primary flight to Air Corps Advanced Flying School. Little did he know what was to come, but he trained his men in perfection.

December 7, 1941 was a Sunday. The United States was bombed at Pearl Harbor in Hawai'i by the Naval Forces of Japan. This act of aggression caused the United States to become involved in World War II.

That very day, I dropped my two aunts off to their friend's house. There was a gal, Doris Lewis, who lived at the Bess Apartment building. I drove around and stopped at the apartment to visit a friend. The apartment was right next to the two houses we owned.

Miss Doris yelled out to me, "I guess you're going to fly after all!"

I had no idea about Pearl Harbor, but I learned fast. The United States was at war, and this war was going to create the opportunity for me to fly.

Some young men enlisted into the armed forces during or right after high school.

The military draft was formed to draft young men into military service. We would need a very large army to fight the war. The soldiers we already had weren't enough. Many civilian organizations were formed to be a part of the aiding of the war effort. It affected everyone. We had rations for food and gas. We had things like the Red Cross, bomb shelter wardens, medical help services, and the Civil Air Patrol.

The Civil Air Patrol (CAP) were civilian pilots utilized for aiding in the war effort. They were spotters. They helped train young people in the aviation subjects.

Frank (center) in his Civil Air Patrol uniform

I signed up for the Civil Air Patrol as soon as I could.

This was my very first opportunity to learn all about all areas of flight. I joined the Civil Air Patrol as a cadet.

I was still in high school. I attended CAP classes in the evening after I left work at Jack Hanthorn's garage. Of course, I went home, cleaned up, and ate supper. I was kind of busy. I didn't care. It was a step toward my goal.

Frank with neighbors after church

I believed in working toward my goals. I enjoyed the chance. I rarely slept. Was it perfect? No, but it was opportunity.

Do we ever reach perfection? Well, it depends on your interpretation. Not anyone else's.

I look at it this way. If we had stopped at the horse and buggy, the automobile would not be here today. If the Wright Brothers' flight at Kitty Hawk was good enough, we would not have sent men to the moon. Chuck Yeager would not have broken the sound barrier.

I say, "Never say never."

You might be proven wrong on some things, but some time you might just be the one to invent, improve, help, or learn something that contributes to our world.

Sorry, I got carried away. Back to high school.

The long and short of it: the Civil Air Patrol taught me to fly.

Sunday photos for Mama and Aunt LaLa

While I learned to fly in the Civil Air Patrol, things changed fast in Tuskegee. By January 11, 1942, five cadets entered advanced flight using AT-6 aircraft.

Funny thing was I never told Mama I learned to fly. She thought I was just learning about flight. She didn't understand I was actually flying.

One day I was in my bedroom adding up my flight time in my log book. Mama walked in, and that was it.

She said, "What is that all about?"

Mama fumed when she realized that I had been flying airplanes. It scared her to death that I wanted to fly.

She said, "As long as you live in this house, you will not fly in an airplane!"

Frank's senior portrait

My response was, "I'll just go live with Pops, my grandfather."

I knew that was the right button to push. Mama and Aunt LaLa were less than fond of Pops. He was quite a "rounder" as they used to say. That meant he liked the ladies.

Mama gave me a big "humph" and stormed out of the room.

As you can guess from the title of this book, I won that little battle with Mama. I continued with the Civil Air Patrol. From that day forward, Mama bragged that her son was going to be a pilot.

Dorothy Jones and Leo Schuth continued to instruct me in flight. We started by holding the controls.

Eventually they started saying Tuskegee would have Civilian Pilot Training (CPT). Like I said before, I had never heard of Tuskegee. The guys and Dorothy at the Civil Air Patrol showed me the Tuskegee Institute in the flight magazine. They said I should go. The government would pay for my college.

I'm thrilled to say I completed my senior year of high school. Yes, I graduated. Right as I graduated from high school, the third class graduated from flight training at Tuskegee.

Now I can't end my high school career without telling you one last high school story.

Bobby Saunders and I drove up to Denver. We attended my cousin's prom. We promised Mama and Mrs. Saunders we'd be back by the time of our baccalaureate and graduation practice.

Bobby and I were right on schedule, heading south on the old 83 highway from Denver. The next thing I know, the steering wheel came right off the shaft in Bobby's Chevy. Bobby steered alright. The problem was that the wheel ended up an arm's length above his head. I am not joking.

Good thing for us, Bobby knew how to slow down using the brakes. I am pleased to say we did not get hurt, but we missed out on graduation practice. Both of our families were in attendance, ready to watch. We showed up with about seven minutes left.

You can just imagine the chewing out we got for that one.

We graduated anyway. It was 1942.

CHAPTER 14

Tuskegee

E vents were moving along for me. I soloed for the first time with the Civil Air Patrol. I will say it was far more successful than jumping off the chicken coop. Pine Valley is the airfield where I soloed. Today, it is the airfield for the United States Air Force Academy. At age ninety-two, I flew my birthday flight from that very same airstrip. It was a spectacular day! The air was as smooth as glass.

Back in 1942, the world was moving fast. World War II consumed the country, and advances in aviation happened at tremendous speed.

You might think it strange that I had never heard of Tuskegee. Thankfully, Dorothy Jones

Frank's 92ⁿᵈ birthday flight–the same airfield where Frank completed his first solo flight as a teenager in the Civil Air Patrol

and Leo Schuth had heard of it. They were true aviators. They understood I wanted to be a pilot, too. Remember, Dorothy gave me flying lessons in high school. Both she and Leo said I should apply to Tuskegee. I could get trained to be a licensed pilot and go to college. It was called Civilian Pilot Training (CPT).

I could get my flying experience free, but I would have to take these tests to get in. So, that's what I did. I went up to the New Customs House in Denver to take the tests. Thankfully, the tests were about mechanical things. With a score above seventy-five, you could apply for the CPT. I don't know what my scores were, but they were over seventy-five. They tried to put me in the Air Corps. That meant the military. I told them I wanted to do the CPT in college, so they switched it.

There's a funny thing I remember about all this testing: Dr. Woodard. He gave some of the physicals. Every time I went to his office to get a physical, he would see me.

"Don't I know you? You Rosie's kid?"

"No, sir," I reminded him. "I'm Maude's son. I used to cut and water your lawn. Shined your shoes, too."

He remembered for a moment. Next trip to get a physical, we started the same conversation again. For as smart as he was, he couldn't remember a face.

September approached. I got all my papers and whatnot. I put my age up. That means that I said I was older than I was. A lot of young men did this to enter the war efforts. At the New Customs House, my age never came up. I had just turned eighteen, but I was supposed to be twenty or something like that to get into the CPT program, college, and flight school.

Off I went. I was excited. I headed to Tuskegee.

I started a class on aircraft mechanics. I was so busy I never wrote or called home. Back then, calling from one state to another was like calling the moon. It just never occurred to me.

Lucky for me, I visited Dr. Carver's lab. That's right. Dr. George Washington Carver. If you don't know who he is, you should look him up, too! Tuskegee still has his lab and a museum.

I'd go in and ask him questions about stuff. He was more agricultural than mechanical. That didn't matter to me. Dr. Carver was an innovator. That lab was a wonderful place for me.

Dr. George Washington Carver

If you didn't know, Henry Ford, the inventor of one of the first cars, came to Dr. Carver on more than one occasion. Henry Ford needed automobile paint. Dr. Carver worked and worked to come up with good automobile paint. Then it was plastics. Henry Ford tried to get Dr. Carver to go up to Detroit. Dr. Carver wanted to stay right where he was at Tuskegee.

Every once in a while, Dr. Carver would disappear for days. Everyone on campus knew where he was. He went out in the woods and talked to God. He came back having figured out all kinds of things.

I walked past him on the campus. He always dressed in a suit coat. He was tall and skinny.

Dr. Carver would always say, "Hello, hello, hello" in a high-pitched voice.

He never would accept money for his work.

He always said, "Give it to the college."

I'm grateful I visited him. I'm not even sure I appreciated his gift for discovery or knew how important he was to our world. He passed away during the months I was back home in Colorado.

You might think it was easy from this point on. Well, you'd be wrong.

I busied myself in Dr. Carver's lab and my mechanics classes. I had only been in Alabama a couple of weeks. I never wrote home.

Mama called the school because she was worried about me. She told them, "Our poor little boy, we haven't heard from him. He's never been away from home before."

As the conversation went on, Mama ended up ratting me out on my age. Not on purpose, but she did. They never asked for a birth certificate or anything. Good thing I didn't have one yet.

Jimmy Plinton was from New York City. I say that because he was a true New Yorker.

He called me into the office. "I just heard from your folks. They said you just turned eighteen. You're too young."

Jimmy Plinton at Moton Field

"Son, we have to send you home," he said.

My world fell apart.

Mama sent money to get me home. Usually, I was good at managing my funds. On this trip home, I wasn't. I just didn't care. I bought some items before leaving Tuskegee and ended up going a day and a half on the train without food.

I learned my lesson. I was so hungry by the time I reached Colorado Springs, I left my bags at the station and walked straight home. I went back later to get them, after I ate.

Next day after I got home, I marched directly to Jack's.

After a few choice words about why I was there, Jack said, "What you waiting for? Get to work."

I really didn't know what I was going to do. I still wanted to fly.

Jack used to say, "If you'd leave those airplanes alone, you'd make a halfway decent mechanic."

I heard that from a lot of people.

I was grateful to be working at Jack's, but I was discouraged. I wanted to be a pilot.

A few months passed. That April, the first group of pilots trained at Tuskegee packed for overseas combat.

Salute and review of the first class of Tuskegee cadets

By June, the Ninety-ninth encountered German Fighters while escorting twelve A-20's over Pantelleria Island. In the meantime, I was home studying my old chemistry, physics, and math books from high school.

My dyslexia was still a problem, but I was getting a handle on it. While I was home, I studied and studied. I knew what I had to do. After a couple of months, I would retake all those tests and try again.

By July 2, 1943, Lt. Charles B. Hall earned the first Tuskegee aerial victory. He shot down a FW-190. World War II engulfed the country.

Eventually I would have to sign up for the draft, so I headed back to the New Customs House and retook the test. I scored even higher. This time I did enter the Army Air Corps. That way they couldn't send me home for my age. You see, Civil Air Patrol at Tuskegee trained civilians. Army Air Corps at Tuskegee trained military.

I stayed home for Christmas, then headed off on December 28, 1943. They sent me to Keesler Field for basic training, and back to Tuskegee I went. Ol' Jimmy Plinton still worked in the office when I showed up a year later.

He said, "What you doing here? I thought I sent you home."

I told him, "I'm here to fly. You can't send me home this time. I'm in the Army Air Corps."

I had to go to college before flight school. I attended the College of Tuskegee.

They retested me. I did even better. I figured out how to read the questions first, then read the article. It helped me find the correct answers.

Of course, when it came to mechanics, that was easy. They had psycho-motive and psychological tests. I got through all that in three or four months. It should have taken two years. With a two-year diploma in hand, they sent me to Maxwell Field.

Eventually, I got into cadet proper. Finally, I trained to fly.

I was thrilled.

You might think I felt perfectly at home. In truth, I was an outcast. I had a terrible time at first.

Two simple reasons. Most of my classmates were really book smart. I was not, as you know. I was mechanical. Reading still haunted me.

The other reason? You might think it strange. Tuskegee was the first time in my life I noticed all the segregation.

I had grown up in a neighborhood where color did not matter. I thought I could do anything. Many of my classmates had a different idea. They told me I couldn't do this or that.

I didn't listen. I wanted to fly, and that's what I was going to do.

Lt. Noel Parrish Commander,
Tuskegee Army Airfield

To get along with classmates, I spent time explaining the mechanics of the aircraft. That's how I started to fit in with the other cadets. They helped me with the book work, and I helped them with the mechanics.

By this time, September 1943, the War Department announced training of "Negroes as bomber pilots." This proved a tremendous breakthrough. All my fellow aviators who trained at Tuskegee jumped at the chance. Being a fighter pilot, well, that was top notch. I can tell you the world would not be disappointed. Some of the greatest flyers were given an opportunity.

Now you know I could already fly, but I never told that to anyone during flight school.

One day in primary, I was up flying. I hot dogged around. While we practiced, we memorized the locations of all the bootleggers from the smoke. The town of Tuskegee was in Macon County. It was what was called a "dry" county. That meant no selling of alcohol. However, "bootlegging," or the making of moonshine, was in full swing. Now you might think this has nothing to do with flying, but it did. We never used radios or air control until later years. The smoke from those old bootleggers helped us with our directions. That's how we navigated back to the airfield. We followed the smoke.

I was doing some aerobatics and lost my bearings. I remembered this old bootlegger. I knew exactly how far he was from the airfield, so I followed his smoke. Well, it was the wrong bootlegger. I was too far out and running out of fuel.

I had to figure it out fast. I would run out of gas soon, so I landed on the cotton side of the field. I did not want to damage the aircraft. The corn stalks were tall and dry. They would tear holes in the fabric. Worse, those corn stalks could flip the plane. If that fabric was torn, they would disassemble the plane to get it out of the corn field and back to Moton Field. Back then, the airplane wings were covered entirely in fabric.

I set that plane right down, and the farmer came right out there. They took me in and they called the base. I told them I could fly it back with a little fuel, but my instructors said, "Oh, no. That's not happening."

They drove out to retrieve me.

To Frank–A thank you note from a Korean Veteran

They had no idea I had been flying for a couple of years.

A different day in primary, a big wind storm came up. I was heading in to land. We were in bi-planes at that level of training. They were called PT-17's. We landed according to the tetrahedron arrows that were placed near the airstrip.

As I approached, I thought to myself, "They didn't turn that thing to face into the wind. I have to make a crosswind landing." Fortunately, I learned how to do that back home.

I slipped that airplane in and kept the wing down. The cross wind blew hard, but nothing like the Eastern slope in Colorado. In the meantime, everyone lined up alongside the hangar.

I thought, "What on earth are they doing out there?"

I landed, and everyone ran out to grab the plane. It was that windy.

We rode the bus back to campus.

My classmates said, "Boy, we thought you were going to crash."

I responded, "I didn't think that wind was so bad." I told them where I'm from we have so much wind we have what's called a "Wyoming wind sock."

"What's that?" they chimed.

I told them, "It's a telephone post with a log chain fastened to it. We only worry when the chain links start flying off."

The boys from Denver laughed so hard they were almost crying.

We all knew how to fly in the wind. The guys who grew up on the Eastern slopes of the Rocky Mountains learned to fly in the wind every day. The Civil Air Patrol taught us that.

I suggest you look up other flyers, like Wendall Pruitt. He maneuvered an airplane like no other. If you watch the movie *Red Tails*, they talk about him. He was one of the Gruesome Twosome flight team.

North American P-51 Mustang

Now I progressed from primary all the way up to advanced flight training. By this time, some of my fellow Tuskegee aviators were flying overseas.

Once again, I hit a setback.

I'm not telling you these things for you to feel sorry for me. I'm telling you because I want you to know you can overcome hardship.

I headed out for the day's training. We were up there having a blast. We loved practicing our dog fighting. That's when you practice shooting down the enemy aircraft. When you are a fighter pilot, you think you can do almost anything. I flew beautifully. I had a terrible head cold, but I knew I was close to graduation. I wanted to get in as much flying as possible. I didn't want to miss my turn in the sky. Looking back, I should have gone to the dispensary. That's the doctor. Being stubborn, I didn't.

Frank's class, 45-A. Frank sits front row, far left with his arms
wrapped around his legs

We maneuvered out there like a Hollywood version of dog fighting. Dog fighting is strictly forbidden until after graduation and you proceeded to combat training.

I pulled some maneuver, and **_pop!_** I blew out both of my eardrums.

Needless to say, I spent the next year recovering. I was so close to graduation my officer's uniform hung neatly in my locker, ready for the ceremony.

They sent me to radio codes school. They hoped it would aid in restoring my hearing. It did help to some degree. Finally, I recovered and finished.

By the time my ears were better, the war had ended.

My classmates called me T-6. That is my favorite plane.

Frank in flight gear during primary training

The last class at Tuskegee was 46-C. They completed training on June 29, 1946.

We all tell a different story.

We faced obstacles. For me, dyslexia proved the toughest.

We conquered hardship. For me, not knowing my mother and father pained me.

We tackled opportunity. For me, flight opened doors.

Most importantly, we "made something of ourselves."

If I can, then you can, too!

About the Authors

Franklin J. Macon is a Documented Original Tuskegee Airman and dyslexic. He grew up and still resides in Colorado Springs, Colorado.

Frank's wish is for all kids to live with purpose and conquer their challenges.

What makes Frank an expert? Ninety-four years of life accomplishments and history.

Tuskegee Motto
1. Aim high
2. Believe in yourself
3. Use your brain
4. Never quit
5. Be ready to go
6. Expect to win

Elizabeth G. Harper grew up in Hudsonville, Michigan and now resides in Colorado Springs, Colorado with her husband, Lew, a retired Air Force Lt. Colonel, and children, Hannah and JB.

Elizabeth works with troubled and adjudicated kids and has spent over twenty-five years in education.

Driving home from Frank's 92nd birthday flight at the United States Air Force Academy, Frank said to Liz, "All those reporters say I should write a book. They always say that."

That day, August 25, 2015, Frank and Liz decided why not?

Project Instructions

Skeezix Parachute

Required Materials:

1 Square of Fabric, Plastic, or a Handkerchief
1 Rock or Army Man
1 ball of string

1. I used a square of fabric. You could use plastic or a handkerchief as well. You can also try some different materials.
2. For my load, I would use rocks when I wasn't using my Skeezix. I think using an army man would be fun.

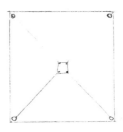

Can you come up with a way to launch a parachute from a model rocket? That way, you can attach an army paratrooper and watch him go.

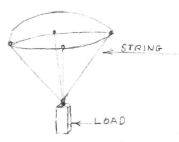

Chugs

Required Materials:

2"x4" Wood Material   1 Orange Crate

4 Wagon Wheels   1 Rope

1. We used the 2"x4" material for the frame. As for distance between the wheels, we used whatever was available. We never measured anything. We eyeballed it, as you would say. We were "eyeball" engineers.
2. I would estimate about 3' for the cross, and for the length, I would estimate about 4-5'. We used whatever we had available.
3. The seat and back came from an orange crate.
4. The wheels we used were from our wagons or skates. Whatever we could find.
5. A rope was our steering device, as well as our feet on the 2"x4" front axle frame. The brakes were our heels. That's why our shoes didn't last very long. I wonder why?

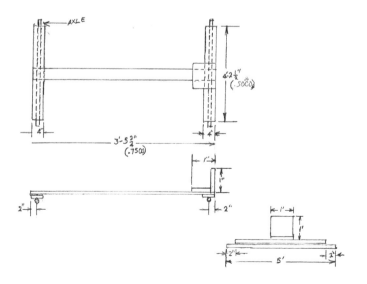

6. The axles the wheels rotated on were usually nailed to the underside of the 2"x4" front axle. We drove the nails in part way and then bent the nail around the axle.

As old folks would say, "Po folk have po ways, but they find a way to make them work." And so do ten-year-olds. You may ask, "Did the axle rods come loose?" **_Yes!_** How do you overcome that problem? Simple. Add more nails.

Can and String Telephone

Required Materials:
2 Cylinder-shaped Oatmeal Containers
1 Kite String

1. To make a telephone, we used two cylinder-shaped oatmeal containers. In the center of the bottom of the oatmeal containers, make a very small hole.
2. Run a long length of kite string through the hole. Run it to the other end of the second oatmeal container. Tie a knot at each end so the string will not slip out.
3. Stretch the string taught.
4. Place the open end of the oatmeal container to your ear, with your friend at the other end. One person talks into the open end of their oatmeal container. The other listens. To answer, have your friend put the oatmeal container to their ear, while you talk into yours.

Question: What causes the voice sound to travel down the string and into the other oatmeal container? First, think about it. See what you can figure out, and then look it up.

Scooters

We constructed two types of scooters. One was using an orange crate. This is the other type of scooter.

Required Materials in 1925:
1 2"x4" Wood Material
1 2"x2" Wood Material
2 Roller Skates

1. It used one 2"x4" board. It was for the base. It was about 2' long. The up-right or vertical board is about 3' high.
2. Two roller skates were used as wheels. Today, I would surely use skateboard wheels instead of roller skate wheels. We attached the skates by using nails. We pounded them in part way and then bent the nails around the skate to hold them onto the base board. It was crude, but it worked for us.
3. The dimensions are not fixed. They are based on your height. Figure out what suits you the best.

Orange Crate Scooter Materials Required in 1925:
1 2"x4" Wood Material
1 2"x2" Wood Material
2 Roller Skates
1 Orange Crate

1. Cut 2"x4"x56". Mount the orange crate vertically so the box is flush with the end of the 2"x4" and centered onto the bottom of the orange crate.
2. On the top of the orange crate, mount the handle bar. To make the handle bar, cut the 2"x2" long enough for your hands. Go past the box top, or about 18" or 19" overall. You

can take a pocket knife and whittle the two round ends to fit your hand grip.

3. Mount the old skates on the underside of the 2"x4"x36". For either base, use the one skate in front and the other skate in the back. Turn both skates so the heels are against the end of the 2"x4". This way, you have good support for both skates. (Today, I would use skateboard wheels for this, too.)

The dimensions are not fixed. Just use what is good for you. The orange crate scooter's base was about 24" longer than the box. These dimensions are only to give you a starting point.

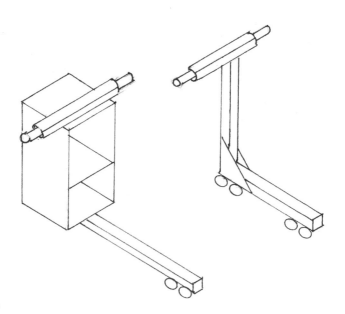

Crystal Set Radio

You may find several ways to make a crystal radio. This is the way we made ours.

Required Materials:
Galena Crystal (Today, you can get a diode. We used to order them from Radio Shack. Now, you can use the Internet to order them).
Headset
Copper Wire (Single-strand)
Mounting Board
Outside Antennae (The longer the antennae, the better the reception.)

1. This is the crystal and mount.
2. The wire attached to the antennae side is called a "cat whisker." It is used to search for the radio station signals. You move it around the crystal to find the radio signal.
3. This is where the outside antennae is attached and goes out the window.
4. The ground post attaches to this lead. The ground can be attached to a water pipe in the house or a metal rod driven into the ground outside your window.
5. These are the posts your headphone leads are attached to.
6. These are your headphones.

All copper wire is single-strand. Except the antennae. It was multi-strand for greater strength. The antennae (3) wire should be non-shielded with insulators on both ends to prevent the antennae from being grounded. The lead wire from the antennae must also be shielded going under the window into the house. This is to prevent grounding by the house. The lead-in wire from the ground also passes into the house. I ran my antennae from the garage to the house, which was quite a long distance. That gave me very good reception.

This is one way I made a crystal radio set. I made it as I was learning about radio reception. Use your imagination. Come up with different configurations as we did. However, this is the simple one. Later on, we made coils by wrapping bare copper wire around oatmeal containers. This also increased our reception. Have fun!

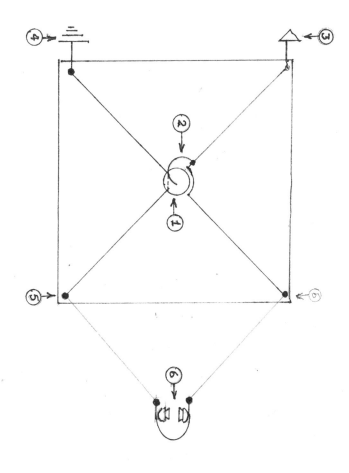

Spool Tractors

Many of the toys we made were out of old spools. Bobby and I made what we called "tractors." I made a couple for you to see. They are fun.

Required Materials:
1 Spool
1 Short Stick (We used kitchen matchsticks.)
1 Long Stick
1 Rubber Band
1 Washer or Button (A piece of wax works, too.)
(Optional) Thumbtack (So the short stick won't slip.)

1. Put the rubber band through the spool.
2. Slide the stick in the rubber band.
3. Hold the spool and spin the long stick. When the rubber band is wound up, set your tractor on the ground and watch it go.

Just remember, you may have to make some alterations. We did. Our first tractors were like the pictures. We carved notches for better traction after a few trial runs.

Gear Ratios and Spools

I would not recommend doing this to your wall like I did. You will get into **_big_** trouble. I would suggest a smaller version. It will teach you the same principles.

Here, I made one to show you. It works the same way.

Required Materials:
1 12"x10" Fiberboard
6-10 Spools (various sizes)
6-10 Nails
5-10 Rubber Bands
1 12" String or Rope
6-10 Washers (A washer between the mounting board and spools serves to reduce drag.)

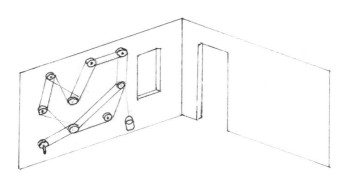

Orange Crate Airplanes

Required Materials:

2 Orange Crates
4 Wagon Wheels
1 2"x2"x8' Board
1 Bamboo Pole

1. We used an orange crate for this experiment. The wings were bamboo poles. Bamboo was available as they were used for clothes lines. Everyone hung their clothes out to dry on the clothes line. The bamboo poles helped hold up the clothes line. Washing machines and dryers were not available at that time.

2. I do not recall our first plane having a tail section or wing struts. That is probably why the first plane fell to pieces. I was the test pilot.

3. The wings were covered with newspaper and flour paste. That is what we used to make our kites as well.

4. We discovered a few design flaws when we launched our flying machine down the hill. The one main flaw was that the wings came off and the newspaper covering was not the 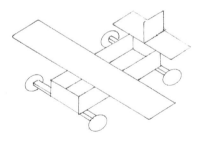 best choice. It ripped. Back to the drawing board.

Our second plane looked like the one I drew for you at the top of the page. Our parents found out about the flying machine and strongly requested we give up the idea of flight. We thought, "How dare they stand in the way of progress!"

Kites

We made our own kites from scratch.

Required Materials:
2 Strips of Wood (1 short, 1 long)
1 String
2 Newspapers torn in Strips
1 Bucket of Glue (made from flour and water)
3 Strips of Material for a Tail

1. We cut strips of wood from an orange crate. We tied one short wood strip and one long strip together. They looked like a cross.
2. We ran string all the way around the outside edges of the wood.
3. We glued the paper around the string. The paste was made from kitchen flour and water. We almost always used the Sunday funny papers. If you don't know what the funnies are, I will tell you. That was the section in the newspaper that had all the comic strips. We used this part because it was colorful.
4. Fold the paper over the string. Apply very light amounts of your homemade paste. Today I would use a glue stick. Very neatly fold it over the string. It will take a while for the paste to dry.
5. Add a tail. The longer the tail, the more stable the kite.

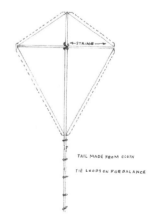

Have fun with your homemade kite. They fly much better than the ones from the store. Why? You made it yourself.

Box Kites

Here is a drawing of a box kite. This type of kite I have seen flying. I think it would be great to experiment with. Look on your computer; there are several kites you can make. Use the same types of materials and principles we used in the 1920's.

This is another picture I drew. Do an experiment to see what works the best.

Again, the longer the kite tail, the more stable most kites are during flight.

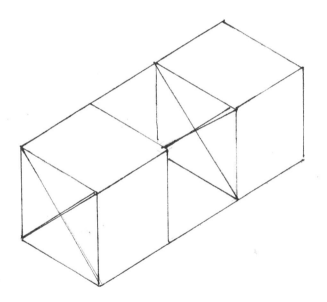

The Principal of Aerodynamics

You can amuse your friends with this trick. To understand the principal of aerodynamics (flight), you can experiment with a simple empty spool of thread. To do this experiment, you will need the following:

1 4"x4" Square Stiff Piece of Paper
1 Spool
1 Straight Pin

1. Locate the center of the paper square by drawing a line from the opposite corners. It will look like an X.
2. See? Here is my example. Where the lines intersect (cross) will be the center. Insert the straight pin all the way until the head of the pin is flush with the bottom of the paper. Place the spool so the pin goes through the hole in the spool. Now you may hold the paper flat on your hand.
3. Blow through the hole on the top of the spool. Remove your hand from the paper. The paper will stay up with the spool if you blow hard through the hole.

Question? Why does the paper not fall to the ground when you are blowing hard?

Answer: The fast-moving air across the top surface of the paper eliminates most of the air pressure. The air pressure on the lower surface supports the paper. This is why a wing on an airplane can support the aircraft in flight. The air pressure on the top surface is less because it is moving faster than the air on the lower surface of the wing.

Do you want to know why the air on top is moving faster? Well, ***look it up!***

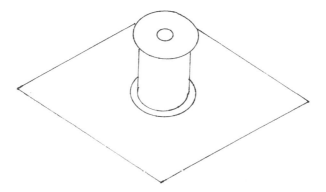

Photo Acknowledgements

Introduction:
1. Medal front – Courtesy of Deanna Dyekman, Joyful Traditions, LLC
2. Medal back – Courtesy of Deanna Dyekman, Joyful Traditions, LLC
3. Frank by AF plane – Courtesy of United States Air Force Academy Public Affairs Office

Chapter 1:
1. Frank infant – Franklin Macon personal collection
2. Eva with dog – Franklin Macon personal collection
3. Family Bible – Courtesy of Deanna Dyekman, Joyful Traditions, LLC
4. Eva adult – Franklin Macon personal collection
5. Frank and Eva – Franklin Macon personal collection
6. Back Porch – Franklin Macon personal collection
7. Parachute – Franklin Macon personal collection
8. Alexander Aircraft – Courtesy of Peterson Air Force Base Air and Space Museum
9. Jimmy Donohue poster – Courtesy of Peterson Air Force Base Air and Space Museum

10. Smithsonian National Air and Space Museum (NASM2018-00196)
11. Charles Lindbergh, Unidentified Artist, 1927, Gelatin silver print National Portrait Gallery, Smithsonian Institute

Chapter 2:

1. Clara – Franklin Macon personal collection
2. Bessie Coleman license – Smithsonian National Air and Space Museum (NASM 99-15416)
3. Bessie Coleman – Smithsonian National Air and Space Museum (NASM 93-16054)
4. Frank in the Garden – Franklin Macon personal collection

Chapter 3:

1. Frank with violin – Franklin Macon personal collection
2. Buck Rogers – Public domain
3. F4F-4 Wildcat – Photo by Eric Long, Smithsonian National Air and Space Museum (NASM 98-15877)
4. Chug – Franklin Macon personal collection
5. Edison fuse – Public domain
6. Eva – Franklin Macon personal collection

Chapter 4:

1. Mama, LaLa, Frank – Franklin Macon personal collection
2. William J. Powell – Smithsonian National Air and Space Museum (NASM 2000-10698)
3. Shoe X-ray – Public domain

Chapter 5:

1. Chicken coop – Franklin Macon personal collection
2. Frank and Ruth – Franklin Macon personal collection

3. FM-1 Wildcat – Smithsonian National Air and Space Museum (NASM 90-4387)
4. Civil Air Patrol – Franklin Macon personal collection
5. *Popular Science* – Public domain
6. Carbide – Franklin Macon personal collection
7. Ovaltine ad – Public domain

Chapter 6:

1. Frank with book – Franklin Macon personal collection
2. Frank with hands in pocket – Franklin Macon personal collection
3. Ruth and father – Franklin Macon personal collection
4. Gilmore Gasoline – Public domain

Chapter 7:

1. Mama, LaLa, watertank – Franklin Macon personal collection
2. Carbide rocket – Franklin Macon personal collection
3. Frank dressed up – Franklin Macon personal collection
4. Banning and Allen – Smithsonian National Air and Space Museum (NASM 99-15420)
5. Frank on pony – Franklin Macon personal collection

Chapter 8:

1. Anderson and Forsythe poster – Smithsonian Air and Space Museum (NASM 99-15427)
2. First Lady E. Roosevelt and Chief Anderson – Public domain
3. Scooter – Franklin Macon personal collection
4. Crystal set radio – Franklin Macon personal collection

Chapter 9:

1. Tractor – Franklin Macon personal collection
2. Spools on the wall – Franklin Macon personal collection
3. Frank demonstrating spools – Franklin Macon personal collection
4. Willa Brown – Smithsonian National Air and Space Museum (NASM 7B01167)
5. Antlers, street car, telegraph building – Courtesy of the Pikes Peak Library District Special Collections (402-44)
6. Railroad bridge – Courtesy of the Pikes Peak Library District Special Collections (001-4574)

Chapter 10:

1. Schwinn bicycle advertisement – Public domain
2. Orange crate airplane – Franklin Macon personal collection
3. B.O. Davis and Tuskegee Airmen – Courtesy of Deanna Dyekman
4. Pops – Franklin Macon personal collection
5. Buffalo soldiers – Public domain

Chapter 11:

1. Jesse Owens, 1936 – Public domain
2. Cornelius Coffey – Smithsonian National Air and Space Museum (NASM 91-6606)

Chapter 12:

1. Frank in cowboy hat – Franklin Macon personal collection
2. Outhouse – Franklin Macon personal collection
3. Frank Loper – Courtesy of the Pikes Peak Library District Special Collections (001-9142)
4. Hindenburg – Public domain

5. Amelia Earhart – Smithsonian National Air and Space Museum (NASM 2009-31377)

Chapter 13:

1. Frank, high school – Franklin Macon personal collection
2. Speaking to cadets – Courtesy of the United States Air Force Academy Public Affairs Office
3. Standing ovation – Courtesy of the United States Air Force Academy Public Affairs Office
4. Frank and Frederick Douglass statue – Franklin Macon personal collection
5. Civil Air Patrol – Franklin Macon personal collection
6. Civil Air Patrol – Franklin Macon personal collection
7. Civil Air Patrol – Franklin Macon personal collection
8. Frank Senior picture – Franklin Macon personal collection

Chapter 14:

1. Birthday flight – Courtesy of the United States Air Force Academy Public Affairs Office
2. George Washington Carver – Public domain
3. Jimmy Plinton at Tuskegee – Franklin Macon personal collection
4. Salute at Tuskegee – Smithsonian National Air and Space Museum (NASM 99-15433)
5. Noel Parrish – Smithsonian National Air and Space Museum (NASM 99-15440)
6. Tuskegee card – Franklin Macon personal collection
7. P-51 Mustang – Smithsonian National Air and Space Museum (NASM 99-15466)
8. Frank's class at Tuskegee – Franklin Macon personal collection

9. Frank in primary – Franklin Macon personal collection

Author Page:
1. Franklin Macon – Courtesy of Deanna Dyekman, Joyful Traditions, LLC
2. Elizabeth Harper – Courtesy of Deanna Dyekman, Joyful Traditions, LLC

Appendix:
1. Skeezix – Franklin Macon personal collection
2. Chug – Franklin Macon personal collection
3. Telephone – Franklin Macon personal collection
4. Scooter – Franklin Macon personal collection
5. Crystal set radio – Franklin Macon personal collection
6. Spool tractors – Franklin Macon personal collection
7. Spool tractor – Franklin Macon personal collection
8. Spools on the wall – Franklin Macon personal collection
9. Orange crate airplane – Franklin Macon personal collection
10. Kite – Franklin Macon personal collection
11. Box kite – Franklin Macon personal collection
12. Aerodynamics – Franklin Macon personal collection

Cover:
1. Franklin Macon – Franklin Macon personal collection
2. Young "Franklin" with wings – Courtesy of Deanna Dyekman, Joyful Traditions, LLC

Back Cover:
1. Young "Franklin" and "Cousin Ruth" –Courtesy of Deanna Dyekman, Joyful Traditions, LLC

Bibliography

Freydberg, Elizabeth, Bessie Coleman. New York: Garland Publishers, 1993.

Hanser, Kathleen. Black Wings: The Life of African American Aviation Pioneer William Powell. Smithsonian National Air & Space Museum, February 2, 1016, https://airandspace.si.edu/stories/editorial/black-wings-lifelafrican-american-aviation-pioneer-william-powell.

Haulman, Dr. Daniel L. "Misconceptions About the Tuskegee Airmen." Air Force Historical Research Agency, 2012.

Haulman, Dr. Daniel L. One Hundred Years of Flight USAF Chronology of Significant Air and Space Events 1903-2002. Maxwell AFB, Alabama: Air University Press, 2003.

Haulman, Dr. Daniel L. "Tuskegee Airmen Chronology." Organizational History Branch Air Force Historical Research Agency, Maxwell AFB, Alabama, 2013.

Haulman, Dr. Daniel L. "Tuskegee Airmen-Escorted Bombers Lost to Enemy Aircraft." Air Force Historical Research Agency, Maxwell AFB, Alabama, 2008.

Headwinds-Early Pioneers/National Air and Space Museum, https://airandspace.si.edu/explore-and-learn/topics/blackwings/index.cfm.

Hilton, Barron, "Pioneers of Flight Gallery," Smithsonian National Air & Space Museum, pioneersoflight.si.edu/people.

Holway, John B. Red Tails, Black Wings: The Men of America's Black Air Force. Las Cruces, New Mexico: Yucca Tree Press, 1997.

Homan, Lynn M. and Reilly, Thomas. Black Knights: The Story of the Tuskegee Airmen. Gretna, Louisiana: Pelican Publishing Company, 2002.

Lambertson, Giles. "The Other Harlem," Air & Space Magazine, March 2010, https://www.airspacemag.com/history-of-flight/the-other-harlem-5922057/

Lampe, Gregory P. Fredrick Douglass: Freedom's Voice, 1818-1845. East Lansing, Michigan: Michigan State University Press, 1998.

Lopez, Donald S. Smithsonian Guides Aviation. New York, New York: Macmillan Press, 1995.

Macon, Franklin J. Interviews with Elizabeth G. Harper. Personal Interviews. Colorado Springs, Colorado, August 2015-April 2017.

Moye, J. Todd. "The Tuskegee Airmen Oral History Project and Oral History in the National Park Service." The Journal of American History 89, no2 (September 2002): 580-587.

Murphy, Major John D. "The Freeman Field Mutiny: A Study in Leadership." ACSC thesis, Air Command and Staff College, March 1997.

"Pioneer Aviator Bessie Coleman Dies in Jacksonville Aircraft Mishap." Florida Aviation Historical Society News, May 1995:5.

"Red Tails." Journal of the Air Force Association Air Force Magazine (March 2016): 34-41.

Rich, Doris, Queen Bessie: Washington, D.C.: Smithsonian Institute Press, 1993.

Spencer, Chauncey E. Who Is Chauncey Spencer? Detroit, Michigan: Broadside Press, 1975.

Morgan James
Speakers Group

www.TheMorganJamesSpeakersGroup.com

We connect Morgan James published authors with live and online events and audiences who will benefit from their expertise.

Morgan James makes all of our titles available
through the Library for All Charity Organization.

www.LibraryForAll.org

CPSIA information can be obtained
at www.ICGtesting.com
Printed in the USA
BVHW032113051218
534639BV00050B/443/P